THE SCHWEICH LECTURES ON
BIBLICAL ARCHAEOLOGY, 1935

THE ORIGINS OF
EARLY SEMITIC RITUAL

THE ORIGINS OF EARLY SEMITIC RITUAL

S. H. HOOKE, M.A.

Samuel Davidson Professor of
Old Testament Studies in the University of
London

THE SCHWEICH LECTURES
OF THE BRITISH ACADEMY

1935

Wipf & Stock
PUBLISHERS
Eugene, Oregon

Wipf and Stock Publishers
199 W 8th Ave, Suite 3
Eugene, OR 97401

The Origins of Early Semitic Ritual
The Schweich Lectures of The British Academy 1935
By Hooke, S. H.
Copyright©1938 The British Academy
ISBN 13: 978-1-55635-371-0
ISBN 10: 1-55635-371-5
Publication date 3/20/2007
Previously published by The British Academy, 1938

TO
SIDNEY SMITH

PREFACE

IN these lectures an attempt is made to relate the ritual practices of the Hebrews, as contained in the Old Testament, to the larger field of the elaborate rituals of Mesopotamian civilization, and to what we know of the early ritual of Canaan. The great increase of our knowledge of the ancient religious pattern of the Near East which has accrued in recent years from excavation and research has made it possible to set the ritual practices of the Hebrews in a fresh historical perspective. We are now in a position, as never before, to relate the individual elements of the Hebrew cultus, such as the Passover, or the institution of sacrifice, to the larger complex of ritual practices which existed in the ancient Semitic environment of the Hebrews.

In the main these lectures are a development of the position outlined in the series of essays published in 1933 under the title of *Myth and Ritual* (Oxford University Press).

The first lecture is devoted to a survey of the sources from which our knowledge of Mesopotamian ritual is derived and to a description of the general character of the most important types of Mesopotamian ritual. While there is nothing in this lecture which is not already familiar to the experts in this field, a great deal of it is not generally known to students of the Old Testament and is not easily available to them. Since the ancient religion of Mesopotamia is one of the most important factors in the early environment of the Hebrew people, a general picture of Mesopotamian ritual is essential for the purpose of these lectures.

The second lecture attempts to do the same thing for the early ritual of Canaan. The greater part of this lecture is given up to an account of the significance of the new material from Ras Shamra, in which we have for the first time a contemporary source of information concerning early Canaanite myth and ritual. It is hardly necessary to remind readers that very little of the Old Testament evidence for this part of our subject is contemporary, but represents Canaanite practices as seen through the eyes of the religious thinkers of a much later period. Hence the importance of the new material cannot be over-estimated. A great deal of work on the text and interpretation of these new sources has yet to be done before an authoritative edition of the texts for English readers can be possible, but in the meantime the work of M. Virolleaud and other scholars has provided a sufficiently sure basis for such a general account of the meaning of the texts as this lecture attempts to give for the benefit of English readers.

The last lecture attempts to set the principal ritual practices and institutions of the Hebrews, as contained in the Old Testament and the Mishnah, in the perspective of the Mesopotamian and Canaanite pattern described in the first two lectures, to estimate their debt to these sources, and to arrive at some conception of the historical development of Hebrew ritual. The author is fully conscious that the subject of the last lecture requires a far fuller treatment than is possible within the limitations imposed by the lecture form, but hopes to deal more adequately with the field of these lectures in a later book.

Looking back over the twenty years which have passed since the publication of the late L. W. King's Schweich Lectures on the *Legends of Babylon and Egypt in Relation to Hebrew Tradition*, it is interesting to observe that the rapid accumulation of new material has made it possible to apply the same comparative method of study to the ritual of the ancient Near East as to its myths. As a result it is becoming clear that in the earliest stages of religion, myth and ritual are inseparably connected, and that their study must be carried on side by side.

We can now see that the debt of the Hebrew people to Mesopotamian culture which Professor King so ably demonstrated in the case of the early Hebrew origin-stories is only a part of the larger debt which they owed to Mesopotamia in matters of religious institutions and of law.

It may not be out of place to add here that the decipherment of the so-called 'Hittite' script, and recent researches into the new sources thus made available, have shown the presence in northern Mesopotamia of a third great cultural influence, ranking with Babylon and Egypt, namely, the Hittite and Hurrian civilization.[1]

It has been suggested that the special character of early Hebrew historical writing, so distinct from anything of the kind in Egypt or Babylon, may be due to Hittite influence,[2] and further knowledge may show that the same influence extends to the field of religion. Hurrian parallels to early Hebrew custom have already been suggested.[3]

Hence the whole trend of modern research in this field tends to emphasize the degree to which the Hebrew people, in the early stages of their history, were under the influence of the culture-pattern dominant in the Near East in the middle of the second millennium B.C. It was not until the beginning of the great prophetic movement in the eighth century B.C. that Hebrew religion began to break away from this dominant culture-pattern and to shape its own distinctive contribution to the history of religion.

But this result of modern research, supplementing, and to some extent superseding, the results of the literary criticism of the documents of the Old Testament, is only now beginning to be recognized, and these lectures are merely a small contribution towards this end.

Footnotes will indicate my indebtedness to other workers in this field. The dedication records my debt to a scholar whose help and encouragement have always been unfailing, and whose great stores of learning and experience are so generously at the disposal of students in the field of Oriental studies.

[1] A Götze, *Hethiter, Churriter und Assyrer*, p. 48 (1936).

[2] Götze, op. cit., pp. 72–4.

[3] Cf. E. A. Speiser, *Ethnic Movements in the Second Millennium* B.C., pp. 44–5; C. H. Gordon, BASOR, lxvi. 25ff. (1937); W. F. Albright, *Archaeology of Palestine and the Bible*, pp. 138f. (1933), *et al.*

Finally, I wish to express my thanks to the British Academy for the honour done me in inviting me to deliver these lectures, and for their indulgence with regard to the tardy appearance of the lectures in print. The delay has been due partly to the pressure of many duties, and partly to the hope which I had entertained of being able to offer in an appendix a translation of the Ras Shamra texts for the benefit of English readers. But there are still so many unsolved problems both in the matter of text and interpretation that it seemed wiser to abandon this project.

For the preparation of the Index I am indebted to the kindness of my friend Miss E. W. Hippisley, S.Th. of King's College, London.

S. H. HOOKE

CONTENTS

LECTURE I

FEW things can be more familiar to the student of the Old Testament than the repeated denunciations of ritual contained in the writings of the Hebrew prophets from Amos to Jeremiah. The last-mentioned prophet was apparently ready to welcome the disappearance from the religion of his people of every ritual element. But such an attitude only bears witness to the extent to which early Hebrew religion was dominated by ritual.

The purpose of these lectures is to relate, if possible, what we know of early Hebrew ritual to the general pattern of religious practice prevailing in Canaan and Mesopotamia during the second millennium B.C. The broad result of the immense advance in our knowledge of the civilization of the ancient Near East derived from excavation has been to demonstrate the dominant influence of Mesopotamia on the culture of Canaan. Hence the plan here followed is to begin our inquiry by a summary of the main features of the ritual life of Mesopotamia, indicating as far as possible the relation between public and private rituals. Then we shall go on to attempt a description of the early ritual of Canaan and to estimate its relation to Mesopotamian ritual, and, finally, we shall endeavour to relate the general pattern of early Hebrew religion to its environment.

It is necessary, first of all, to say something about the sources of our knowledge of Mesopotamian religion. The main body of this knowledge is derived from an ever-increasing mass of ritual texts, ranging from the third dynasty of Ur (c. 2300 B.C.) down to the Seleucid period. The study of this abundant material has shown that from an early date priests and scribes in the principal cult centres were at work organizing and arranging the various types of ritual into collections or series. Many such series, more or less complete, are now available for study, and give us a vivid picture of the place occupied by ritual in every department of public and private life in Mesopotamia.

There are collections of incantation texts, such as the well-known *Maqlû* and *Šurpû* series; the valuable collection contained in Dr. Campbell Thompson's *Devils and Evil Spirits of Babylonia*; and other shorter series. There are large collections of omen-texts, divination and exorcism texts, and many short texts containing rituals for removing bodily ailments, such as toothache and headache. We have also a representative collection of texts containing the rituals for the great seasonal festivals (e.g. Thureau-Dangin, *Rituels accadiens*), and a few difficult but very valuable texts, unfortunately not too well preserved, known as ritual-commentaries, containing, for the instruction of priests, an explanation of the various symbolic acts of a ritual by relating them to the myth which accompanied them. Of great importance, also, for our purpose are the Tammuz liturgies, known to us from the work of Zimmern and Langdon, and now more completely presented in the collection made by P. Maurus Witzel under the title of *Tammuz-Liturgien und verwandtes* (1935).

We owe the preservation of much of this invaluable material to the pious activities of Asshurbanipal, who founded a great library at Nineveh, and in whose correspondence are mentioned the names of many series of rituals existing in his day, some of which we possess, while others are only known from his references to them. In a letter, usually attributed to Asshurbanipal, a scribe, Šadunu, is ordered to collect and send to the king copies of a number of ritual texts whose titles are indicated in the letter. The following is a translation of the letter:

'Order of the king to Šadunu: I am well, may your heart be of good cheer. The day you see my letter, Šumâ, the son of Šumukina, Bêlêṭir, his brother, Aplû, the son of Arkatilâni, and such people of Borsippa as you know, take with you, and all the tablets that are in their houses and all the tablets laid up in the temple of Ezida seek out, and collect the tablets for royal amulets (?) of the female chanters for the days of the month Nisan, the amulet of the chanting priests of the month Tashritu, of the incantation series Bit-Sala', the amulet of the chanting priests for reckoning the day, the four amulets for the head of the royal bed, and favourable to the king, box-wood ? cedar for the head of the royal bed. Incantation "May Ea and Marduk complete wisdom", all the series that there are relating to war, the series "In battle a shaft shall not come near a man".

'The series . . . (EDIN. NA DIB. BI. DA. E. GAL TU. RA nipišaanu SU. IL. LA. KAN-a-nu) . . . entering the palace, spells, prayers, stone inscriptions, and those that are favourable for (my) royalty, purification rites for the city, "Turning the eyes" (IGI. NIGIN NA) although this is a trouble, and whatever may be necessary in the palace, as much as there is and the rare tablets on the route, that are not found in Assyria, seek out and bring to me. Now I have sent to the šatanu and the šaku-officials. You shall put these tablets in your strong box. No one shall withhold tablets from you, and if there be any tablet or spell which I have failed to mention to you, and you perceive that it is good for my palace, search for it and get it and bring it to me.' [1]

In addition to these direct sources of information concerning the nature of Mesopotamian ritual there are also a number of indirect and contributory sources.

In his Schweich Lectures on *Babylonian and Egyptian Legends* the late L. W. King pointed out the important fact, whose bearing has been increasingly recognized by modern scholars, that the Babylonian myths, especially in their earlier forms, have a distinct ritual significance.[2] Hence it is possible to find in those myths which have been preserved, such as the Creation myth in its various forms, the myths of Adapa and Etana, the Gilgamesh Epic,[3] and fragments of other myths, important indications of ritual practices.

[1] Leroy Waterman, *Royal Correspondence*, xx. 213. In another letter from the court astronomer Asaridu this official informs the king as follows: ' I have obtained an old inscription which was made by King Hammurabi, and an inscription which is even earlier than King Hammurabi, and I am bringing them with me to Babylon. Then the king can proceed with the ceremonies.' Harper, ABL, no. 18, Rs. 1 ff.

[2] L. W. King, *Legends of Babylon and Egypt*, p. 50 f., *et al.* (1916).

[3] We find a mention of an image of Gilgamesh used in the rites of the month Ab. Waterman, op. cit. xvii. 41 (letter 56).

The Babylonian [1] and Assyrian Laws [2] also serve as a valuable source of information concerning those aspects of ritual which enter into the relations between individuals, or between individuals and the state, such as the ordeal, contracts, and marriage.

Also, the Babylonian and Assyrian Chronicles, and the collections of royal correspondence, contain references to ritual practices connected with public affairs.

Then we have in the great number of seals and reliefs from Mesopotamian excavational sites an important indirect source of information. The recent work of Dr. Frankfort and Mrs. van Buren has shown that many of the scenes depicted on early seals are ritual scenes. In this connexion the following passage from Dr. Frankfort's article, ' Gods and Myths on Sargonid Seals ', [3] is worth quoting :

'As to the Babylonian New Year Festival, there is a considerable number of seals figuring events which we know as part of the ritual . . . the fact that some of its ceremonies, or rather, the myths which underlie them, should be figured as designs of good omen on the cylinder seals is hardly astonishing if we remember the fundamental importance of the festival for the well-being of the whole community and its predominant position in the life of the Babylonians. But it is very interesting to note with which kind of texts the seals provide parallels. There are only one or two instances where we are able to refer to *Enuma eliš*. Most of our quotations are from commentaries on the ritual and not from the Epic of Creation. The significance of this circumstance seems to me great; it indicates the limitations of our attempts to explain the seals. The literary form of a myth, even if it is rich in metaphor, is of a very general character indeed as compared with the extreme definition of an image, and therefore the description of a god or of an event can only in exceptional cases be identified with a picture in such a manner that other explanations are excluded beyond a doubt. But the acts of a ritual possess the same precise definition as a picture, and we have, moreover, in the commentaries on the ritual, verbal versions of the very symbolism which finds pictorial expression on the seals. It is therefore

[1] See R. F. Harper, *The Code of Hammurabi* (1904).
[2] See Driver and Miles, *The Assyrian Laws* (1935).
[3] *Iraq*, i. 1, pp. 6–7 (1934).

to ritual texts and not literary texts that we must look for further material explaining the subjects of the seals.'

The importance of this statement for our purpose is obvious. It indicates that while it may not be possible as yet to use the evidence of the seals for such precise details as the name of the god connected with the ritual depicted on any particular seal, it is nevertheless legitimate to regard the scenes on the seals as giving us a general idea of the most important features of the ritual.

Lastly, the many cult objects found in Mesopotamian sites, the structure of Babylonian temples, in spite of the still incompletely solved question of the meaning of the nomenclature of their various shrines and chambers, all help to fill in the details of the ritual picture. It may be added here that the extraordinary scene unveiled by Sir Leonard Woolley's excavation of the death-pit at Ur brings before our eyes a very moving record of ancient ritual in Mesopotamia. Whether it be a royal burial ritual or, as some scholars maintain, a dedication or fertility ritual of unusual significance, it bears witness to the supreme importance of ritual in the life of the ancient inhabitants of Mesopotamia.

While this great mass of evidence, covering a period of about three thousand years, presents an appearance of extreme complexity, it is nevertheless possible to estimate the relative importance of its constituent parts, and to describe the main principles upon which the system rests. For practical purposes it is convenient to divide the various types of ritual practices into the two classes of public and private rituals, although some of the types of ritual are applicable to both of these classes.

By public rituals we mean those which are performed for the benefit of the community as a whole, while private rituals are those which are intended to meet the needs of the individual. The following are the main types of ritual which may be classified as public :

1. *Seasonal Rituals.*
   i. *The New Year Festival.* It is generally recognized by

scholars that this festival from earliest times occupied the central place in the community life of the city-states of Mesopotamia. Evidence goes to show that variations in date and other details existed in local usage before the rise of Babylon to political supremacy produced a unification of practice. But the fundamental ideas underlying these differences remained unchanged throughout the whole history of Babylonian civilization. We shall return to the discussion of these ideas later on.

ii. *The Tammuz Festival.* While this festival, connected with agriculture, seems to have maintained a separate existence from the New Year Festival, it is so closely related to the latter that our discussion of its implications cannot be separated from the discussion of the New Year Festival.

iii. *The Ishtar Festival.* We have evidence for an Ishtar festival in Nineveh, in Asshurbanipal's time, on the 16th of Tebet, when Ishtar went in procession attended by the other gods. The king took part in the procession, apparently clothed as a god. The exact bearing of this ritual is not clear, but there are grounds for surmising that a sacred marriage is implied.[1] As we shall see, the sacred marriage is one of the central elements in the New Year Festival, and it will be discussed under that head.

iv. *Lunar Festivals.* A prayer to Sin, the moon-god (King, *Magic*, i, obv. ll. 14–27), which is immediately concerned with another ritual occasion, namely, an eclipse of the moon, mentions the 30th of the month as a New-moon festival of rejoicing for the reappearance of the moon. There is also a very close connexion of the moon with the omen-literature. In Hammurabi's time the 7th and 15th of the month also had ritual significance, the latter day being known as *šabattum* or *šapattum*, a word which

---

[1] Cf. the implications of the Gilgamesh Epic as to the marriage of Ishtar to the king of Erech; also the marriage of King Lipit-ishtar to the goddess forms part of his deification-ceremony. Cf. Zimmern in BVSGW, lxviii. 5, 1 ff.

passed into Hebrew ritual usage with a different significance. The 28th day, the day of the moon's disappearance, known as *bubbulu*, was also a ritual day. In the
Assyrian period the 1st, 7th, 15th, 21st, and 28th days
of the month, instead of being feast days became unlucky
days, while the 19th, i.e. the 49th from the 1st of the
previous month (seven sevens), had a specially sinister
character. A well-known passage lays it down that on
these days ' the shepherd of the people (i.e. the king)
shall not eat roast meat nor baked bread, he shall not
change the garment that is on his body, he shall not put
on clean clothes, nor bring any offering; the king shall
not go in his chariot, nor give any commands; the seer
shall do no work in the secret place, the physician shall
not attend to the sick, the day is unsuitable for the
carrying-out of any undertaking '.[1]

These are the principal seasonal or recurrent ritual occasions, but there were also a number of other important
rituals of which we have records which concerned the
community as a whole, and we may take as the second
group of public rituals those concerned with the king as
the representative of the community, the shepherd of the
people.

2. *Royal Rituals.*

Here again, much of the ritual which concerns the king
belongs to the New Year Festival, and will be discussed in
connexion with it, but there are several important ceremonies in which the king or his representative took part.

i. *Deification Ritual.* Only one example of this ritual is at
present known to us, the deification ritual of King Lipit-
ishtar, the fifth king of the first dynasty of Isin (2102–
2092).[2] The existence of such a type of ritual, together

---

[1] IVR, xxxii. 28 ff. Cf. Bruno Meissner, *Babylonien und Assyrien*, ii.
62–3 (1924).

[2] H. Zimmern, BVSGW, 1916, VS x. 199, ii. 43 ff. Cf. also the
list of deified kings in M. Witzel, *Tammuz-Liturgien und verwandtes*,

with other points arising out of the New Year ritual, raises questions concerning the relation between the king and the god in Babylonia which will be discussed later.

ii. *Dedication Rituals.* Several examples of this type of ritual have been preserved. The restoration and dedication of temples was a duty of kings, and had an important bearing on the prosperity of the country. We have also a fairly complete text containing the dedication of a ceremonial litter for Ishtar by Asshurbanipal.[1]

iii. *Eclipse Ritual.* An elaborate ritual, with an associated myth, was performed on the occasion of an eclipse of the sun or moon, or some unusual darkness (*attalu*). The king played an important part in this, and the sacred *lilissu* drum was brought out.[2]

iv. *Funerary Ritual.* In his *Tod und Leben* Ebeling has published several interesting texts which seem to be concerned with royal funerary rites. In general, funerary ritual in Mesopotamia was concerned with the purpose of preventing the dead from returning to trouble the living, but the texts just mentioned suggest that royal funerary ritual was connected with the death of a god in the Creation myth.[3]

v. *Propitiation Ritual.* A number of texts show the king as taking part in rituals which come under the larger class of exorcism or incantation rituals, intended to avert or remove the consequences of the anger of the gods with the community on account of some breach of ritual requirements. The New Year ritual includes an important ceremony of this kind.[4]

pp. 16–18 (1935). Idin-dagan as Tammuz, Langdon in JRAS, 1926, pp. 15–17.

[1] F. Martin, TRAB, i.

[2] BR, iv, No. 6.

[3] E. Ebeling, *Tod und Leben nach den Vorstellungen der Babylonier,* pp. 62–5 (1931).

F. Thureau-Dangin, *Rituels accadiens,* pp. 144–5 (1921).

In addition to these there were many other forms of ritual in which the king took part. He consulted the omens with the due forms in connexion with all public undertakings; he had recourse to the *barû*-priest for the interpretation of his dreams; he made use of the usual incantation and exorcism rituals in cases of sickness or other crises, in the same way as a private individual would. Moreover, the acts and behaviour of the king, especially at the New Year Festival, were observed with special care as the source of omens. On the occasion of treaties with other kings we find that there was a specific ritual for the occasion.

We may next refer briefly to a large and important class of rituals which come under the general head of public ritual, although they were not specially concerned with the functions of the king, but belonged rather to the priests and the cult.

3. *Priestly and Temple Rituals.*

Under this head we may include all the rites of daily and seasonal purification of the priests, the shrines of the gods, and the objects of the cult. These subsidiary rites form part of such larger rituals as the New Year Festival. Under the same head we may also mention the recitation and chanting, with the appropriate music of the sacred instruments, of the various prayers and hymns addressed to the gods, as well as the confessional formulae which entered so largely into the Babylonian religious life. An interesting example of the special type of ritual characteristic of the priestly function is the ceremony of *mouth-washing*.[1] This rite was performed for the statues of the gods and reminds us of the Egyptian ceremony of the *opening of the mouth*. A similar type of ritual requiring the special knowledge which was transmitted from one generation of priests to another was the ritual of the making and consecration of the sacred *lilissu* drum.[2]

[1] S. Smith in JRAS, 1925, pp. 37 ff.; H. Zimmern, *Ritualtafeln*. pp. 31–8.
[2] F. Thureau-Dangin, op. cit., pp. 11 ff.

Finally, the evidence at our disposal shows that there was hardly an occurrence in the private life of the Babylonian which did not provide an occasion for some form of ritual. The event of birth, with its attendant circumstances, called for the activities of the *ašipu*-priest to ward off the malice of demons and evil spirits and every form of ill luck from the pregnant mother. All forms of sickness, the toothaches, headaches, and fevers to which the Babylonians seem to have been specially subject, were met by the appropriate ritual. Marriage and burial were surrounded by ritual. The *barû*-priest was consulted and the omens taken before any kind of undertaking.

The mere enumeration of these various ritual practices is enough to show how completely the ancient Babylonian was dominated by the view of life which expressed itself in these ceremonies. But the central importance of the great complex of rituals constituting the New Year Festival suggests that here we may hope to find the underlying principles of the whole system of Babylonian ritual.

The New Year Festival. The texts in which the ritual of the New Year Festival is preserved are for the most part late, and no doubt represent a long period of growth and accretion, and it is possible that some of the constituent elements of the ritual originally existed as separate rituals of local origin. We can, however, by comparison with earlier references, and with the help of the pictorial representations on the seals, and of allusions in the ritual commentaries and myths, determine with some degree of certainty those essential elements in the New Year ritual which have persisted with little change from the earliest period.

i. The first of these is the dramatic representation, in some symbolic form, of the death or slaying of a god. In the Babylonian form of the ritual the dead god is Marduk, and in the ritual commentary VAT 9555, interpreted by Zimmern, Langdon, Pallis, and others, upon which we largely depend for the reconstruction of this part of the ritual, the scene opens with Marduk dead in the 'mountain'.[1] In spite of much obscurity it is at least clear that the death and resurrection of Marduk was enacted in some form or other as an essential part of the New Year ritual at Babylon. The question arises here whether any part of the ritual was performed in secret, as a mystery, and it is possible that the slaying of the god, in some symbolic form, was a cult act carried out in secret. The evidence of the seals strongly suggests that such an act did form part of the ritual. Dr. Frankfort has shown that a group of seals representing ritual scenes can be connected with the texts relating to the New Year Festival. In his own words: 'These (the seals) seem to shew, in any case, that some of the most important beliefs which underlie the New Year Festival in New Babylonian times, and could therefore be traced back, at most, to the period of Hammurabi, existed already under the dynasty of Sargon of Akkad.'[2] In this group we have several seals representing the ritual slaying of a god, or of a *misch gestalt*, a human figure with bestial attributes. It may not be possible from the evidence of the seals to give a name to the slain figure, but this ambiguity is characteristic of the early texts. We also have a representation of a female goddess sitting or kneeling by a mountain in which the slain or imprisoned god is depicted, a scene which corresponds to a description in the ritual commentary of the actions of Zarpanit, Marduk's consort.

It is clear that behind the present form of the myth and ritual of the New Year Festival at Babylon lie many divergent forms of conception of the dying god. We have a text[3] describing the imprisonment of the god Lillu in the underworld, and the lamentation for him of his sister and mother. Then we have abundant evidence of the early prevalence of the seasonal ritual of Tammuz, centring about his death

[1] For the meaning of *ḫuršan*, 'the mountain', as 'the lower world', cf. S. Langdon, *The Epic of Creation*, pp. 34 ff. (1923).

[2] H. Frankfort in *Iraq*, i. 1, p. 21 (1934).

[3] RA, xix.

in the summer solstice, and the mourning of Ishtar. It seems certain that the death of Tammuz was followed by his resurrection.[1] Further, there is evidence to show that Anu and Ellil, in some period of the growth of the cult, suffered the same fate. It is even possible that Gilgamesh belongs to the same class of dying gods, if Professor Langdon's interpretation of No. 8 in his *Babylonian Liturgies* be accepted; I have ventured to suggest elsewhere that the journey of Gilgamesh across the waters of death in the Epic of Gilgamesh, Tablet X, represents a funerary ritual (*Folk Lore*, Sept. 1934). Hence it is a legitimate conclusion from the evidence at our disposal that from the earliest times of Mesopotamian civilization one of the central elements in the ritual was the ritual slaying of a god in some symbolic form.

In the Creation Epic, whose central episodes clearly represent the events of the most important days in the New Year Festival[2] there is no trace of the death and resurrection of Marduk. We have instead the account of the slaying of Tiamat by Marduk, and the subsequent slaying of Qingu for the creation of man. Nevertheless, the death of Marduk was too central an element to be eliminated, and the ritual commentary, as we have seen, shows that the imprisonment of Marduk in the mountain, the mourning of Zarpanit, the use of the Creation Epic as an incantation to restore the dead god to life, the intervention of Nebo, and his conquest of Zu in a ritual contest, remained essential parts of the cult drama of the New Year Festival at Babylon.

Before we pass on to the second main element in the ritual of the New Year Festival it is necessary to discuss the significance of the ritual slaying of a god. As far back as the evidence of excavation takes us, the social organization of Mesopotamia consists of a number of independent city-states with some form of kingship, and we are not in a position to theorize about an agricultural or pastoral state

---

[1] M. Witzel, op. cit., p. 21 ; S. Langdon, *Sumerian Liturgies*, cci, l. 47 (1913). Cf. E. Ebeling, op. cit., p. 45.

[2] Cf. C. J. Gadd, *Myth and Ritual*, pp. 57–8 (1933).

of civilization prior to the urban civilization which excavation discloses. Pictorial evidence from Ur and elsewhere shows the close relation between the king and agricultural or pastoral pursuits, but the main point is that the king is, as far back as our evidence goes, the central figure in the community.

In the early king-lists several of the kings figure as gods in the myths—Tammuz, for instance, and Lugalbanda. Gilgamesh is two-thirds god and one-third man. Further, there is the regular use of the determinative sign for divinity with the names of Babylonian kings. The ritual of the deification of a king, although we have only one example at present, namely, that of King Lipit-ishtar, already referred to, points in the same direction.[1] It may be suggested that the evolution of the ritual passed through the following stages. First, in the earliest stages the king was actually killed by his successor. There is a passage in the Pyramid Texts[2] which can be taken to indicate the actual eating of the slain king by his successor in order to obtain possession of his magic properties. It is also possible that even at this stage different conceptions of the purpose of the ritual had influenced the practice of the killing of the king. The Tammuz ritual can hardly be dissociated from the idea of the dying of vegetation in the summer heats and its revival in the short-lived Eastern spring. There is also the element of the renewed strength of the unconquered sun, rising from the apparent defeat of the winter in the winter solstice, an element which has survived in Mithraism. Another element which has entered into the ritual is the removal, by the slaying of the king, of all the ritual guilt and defilement accumulated during the year, thus freeing the community from its dread consequences. Finally, there is the well-attested motive of preserving the virility and potency of the king by slaying him before his powers wane, and substituting a new and vigorous embodiment of the powers of nature.

[1] See p. 7, n. 2.   [2] Pyramid Texts, §§ 393–414.

Possibly, even in the earliest stage that excavational evidence presents, the ritual slaying of the king had reached the second stage of its development, namely, the substitution of a symbolic act for the actual slaying. The seals which Dr. Frankfort discusses in the article already mentioned suggest a transitional period. We have there four types of what we may call ritual slaying: the slaying of a human figure with the horned cap denoting divine attributes, which may be intended to depict the actual slaying of the king by his successor; the slaying of a half-human, half-bestial figure, which may be taken to indicate that the myth of the slain god was beginning to take shape. It is possible that such figures were represented in the ritual by priests or other individuals, masked and wearing appropriate clothing. Corroboration of this view may be found in such representations, for instance, as those of the participants in the ritual on the well-known Lamashtu tablet, or of the Minotaur on early Greek vases. Then there is the slaying of various animal forms, the bird of Zu, the bull, symbolic of various gods, the lion, the serpent, or even purely mythical forms, such as the seven-headed hydra on Dr. Frankfort's seal from Tell Asmar. The fourth type of symbolic killing occurs in the interesting seals shown in Plates IV f and V a in Dr. Frankfort's article. These represent a god cutting down a tree or trees on the mountain, conventionally depicted, in which a god is imprisoned. This form of ritual, the cutting down of a sacred tree, has connexions with Tammuz,[1] and with the Phoenician god Khaitan.[2] We may also recall the ritual of the laying down and raising up of the sacred _ded_-tree, symbol of the death and resurrection of Osiris.

This stage of the ritual, in which the killing had become a symbolic act, gave rise to various forms of the significant *puḫu* or substitution-ritual, to which we shall have occasion

---

[1] S. Langdon, op. cit. cci, ll. 27–8.
[2] P. Montet, *Byblos et l'Égypte*, pp. 287 ff. (1928).

to refer again later. There is an interesting suggestion[1] that Meskalamdug, whose grave and funerary furniture were discovered by Sir Leonard Woolley at Ur, was the title of the priest who acted the god for the king, in the situation represented by the interments at Ur, and was slain as his substitute. Two other texts may be referred to in this connexion. In the first, Shamash-shum-ukin, the rebellious brother of Asshurbanipal, is said to have died as an atonement 'for them', i.e. for the rebellious vassals who had followed him in revolt against Asshurbanipal.[2] In the second[3] we learn that when Ira-mitti, a king of the first dynasty of Isin, died during the progress of the New Year Festival, the substitute-king, Ellibani, who should have died instead of the king, succeeded to the throne. This aspect of the ritual slaying of the king survived in the Persian Sacaea,[4] and we have echoes of it in both Greek and Roman ritual.

In the last stage of the development of the New Year Festival ritual it is possible that the killing had become purely symbolic and was carried out in mimic representation by masked actors. VAT 9555, ll. 24–6, suggests that the substitute-king was symbolized by a pig.

One more point remains to be discussed in relation to the ritual slaying of the king or god at the New Year Festival. It appears from the combination of the evidence of the Creation Epic and of the ritual commentary on the cult drama that there were two points in the ritual where a killing took place. There is the slaying of Bel or Marduk in the person of a substitute-king or symbolic animal, followed by his resurrection and the subsequent rejoicings. There is also the slaying of Tiamat, the dragon adversary of the younger gods, and her monstrous consort Qingu, by Marduk, followed by the creation of man. It seems certain

---

[1] H. Frankfort, op. cit., p. 12, n. 3.   [2] E. Ebeling, op. cit., pp. 60 ff.
[3] See L. W. King, CEBK, iii, p. 15.
[4] See S. Langdon, 'Babylonian and Persian Sacaea', JRAS, 1924, pp. 65 ff.

that these are two divergent developments of the original ritual of the killing of the king, and we have already seen the ambivalent representation, on the seals, of the slain figure. Time, however, will not allow of the further discussion of this point.

ii. We turn now to the second main element in the New Year ritual, the sacred marriage. Here again the incompleteness of the text containing the account of the festival obliges us to fall back upon other sources. In this connexion Mr. Gadd says: 'About the ritual marriage we have almost no information at all, and yet are assured not merely that it took place, but that it was symbolically of the utmost importance, being in fact the cult-act of the old agricultural religion upon which the fruitfulness of the year depended.'[1] Indeed, we may say that this element in the New Year ritual is better attested from early sources than the ritual slaying of the king. A well-known passage from Gudea's Cylinder B describes the marriage of Bau and Ningirsu, the prosperity produced by the rite, and the subsequent feastings and rejoicings. Statue G of the same king states that the marriage took place at the New Year Festival. In Harper, *Assyrian and Babylonian Letters*, no. 366, there is a description of a Nebo festival held in the month Iyyar. The festival seems to have lasted twelve days like the New Year Festival, but was almost entirely taken up with the various details of the ritual marriage between Nebo and Tašmet. Other texts might be mentioned, but the existence of the rite is well established. We have also the confirming evidence of the seals, and other forms of pictorial representation. Dr. Frankfort (op. cit., Pl. I*b*) has published an early dynastic seal from Tell Asmar in which he sees the ritual wedding of the god and goddess. The symbol of the entwined serpents, familiar to us from the vase of Gudea dedicated to Ningizzida, has been interpreted, both by Mrs. Van Buren[2] and by Dr. Frankfort,[3]

---

[1] C. J. Gadd, op. cit., pp. 55 ff.   [2] E. van Buren, AOF, x. 64 f.
[3] H. Frankfort, op. cit., pp. 9 ff. With regard to the seal shown in

as the symbol of the sacred marriage. It is also possible that the ceremony of the death-pit at Ur combined, as a rite of special efficacy, a sacred marriage and a royal substitution-rite, where both the *Ersatzkönig* and the sacred bride were slain.

The early Sumerian evidence alone is enough to show (*a*) that the rite was connected with the New Year Festival at Lagash as early as the time of Gudea; (*b*) that it was a fertility ritual, intended to promote the fruitfulness, in all senses, of Lagash; and (*c*) that the king participated in the ritual, for it is stated that he entered the temple with the god for the consummation of the rite.

While these two central elements of the New Year Festival ritual may have originated independently, and have continued to exist as distinct rituals, the sacred marriage not being necessarily confined to the New Year, nevertheless, owing to the central importance of the king in the early city-state organization of Mesopotamia, these two essential rites must have united to form the nucleus of the New Year ceremonies at a very early date. The curiously shifting character of the designations of the gods in the early stages of Mesopotamian religion suggests that the vital thing behind these changing shapes of gods is the human figure, the focus of the community's needs and desires and fears, a figure who could die, be married, and undergo ordinary human experiences, but whose experiences were nevertheless of immense significance for those whom he represented. With the progressive development of the religion, the civilization, and the political organization of Mesopotamia, the distinction between the god, the king, and the priest, originally aspects and functions of one individual, became established, but to the end in Babylonian religion and its ritual the king and the god remained closely united; the king is the son of the god and retains many divine attributes. The extravagant figure 5, it should be remarked that Dr. Campbell Thompson interprets this as a representation of the activities of a vampire.

D

expressions of fawning courtiers are only the pale reflections of a time when such epithets represented the real attitude of subjects towards the king, their actual belief in his powers. While the question of the astral element in early Mesopotamian religion raises a problem which there is not time to discuss, it does not affect the main subject of these lectures, namely, the form of the ritual, its development, and the relation between its parts.

There are two more elements in the New Year ritual which call for a brief discussion and are of considerable importance, but they are so closely connected that they may be taken together.

iii. *The Enuma eliš and the Fixing of Destinies.* While, in relation to the development of the ritual, the Creation Epic, in its present form, is clearly secondary, since it accounts for the situation in which Marduk has become the paramount god of Babylon, and the older myth of the slaying of Marduk has been eliminated, nevertheless its place in the New Year ritual is very important. It is a magical incantation of great potency, and is used to defeat the hostile influences which have brought about the death of the god and his imprisonment in the underworld. It does this by the reinvocation of the situation in which Marduk is victorious over his enemies. We shall see later that the use of the *Enuma eliš* in other rituals is an indication of its central importance. It contains a reference to a cult object and to a ceremony of considerable significance in the New Year ritual, namely, the Tablet of Destiny and the ceremony called the Fixing of Destinies. We do not know at present exactly what the Tablets of Destiny were, but we see from the earlier myths that their possession was of great importance and carried with them supreme magical power. Neither do we know what was the nature of the ceremony called the Fixing of Destinies, a rite which was performed during the last three days of the Festival by Marduk, in consultation with Nebo and the other gods, in a place called the chamber of destinies. But it is clear that this

ceremony was the end to which all the New Year ritual
tended. It was, in a literal sense, the making of a New
Year, the removal of the guilt and defilement of the old
year, and the ensuring of security and prosperity for the
coming year. By this ceremony was secured the due func-
tioning of all things, sun, moon, stars, and seasons, in their
appointed order. Here lies the ritual meaning of Creation,
there is a new creation year by year, as the result of these
ceremonies. The conception of creation in this stage of
the evolution of religion is not cosmological but ritual.
It has not come into existence in answer to speculations
about the origin of things, but as a ritual means of maintain-
ing the necessary order of the things essential for the well-
being of the community.

We come now to the last division of the subject to which
this lecture has been devoted, and shall attempt to indicate
briefly the relation of the other classes of ritual activity to the
central ideas and practices which we have found in the New
Year ritual. Next in order of importance to the New Year
ceremonies is the very comprehensive class of ritual activities
carried out by the *mašmašu* or *ašipu*-priests, activities which
embraced every aspect of Babylonian public and private
life.

If the treatment of this part of the subject seems somewhat summary owing to limitations of time and space, it
will be found that some of the ritual problems raised here
are dealt with in another connexion in the two following
lectures.

i. *Exorcism and Incantation Rituals*. The main purpose of
these rituals is apotropaic, or negative. They are intended
either to ward off the attacks of evil demons of various kinds
or to expel them from the individual whom they had taken
possession of and brought sickness upon. Practically every
form of disease and bodily ailment, as well as other forms
of misfortune, were ascribed to the presence of demons, who
were depicted in a very realistic way. We will take as the

first example of one of these rituals a text[1] which contains
the instructions for dealing with the case of a sick man who
has been attacked by an *utukku* or *saghulḥaza-demon*. The
general pattern of these rituals does not greatly vary, and
usually consists of an invocation to a god or gods, in some
cases a confession, and a series of cult acts, sometimes quite
short and simple, sometimes long and complicated, constituting the ritual proper. The ritual is usually accompanied
by a spell to be recited by the officiating priest.

In this ritual, appointed to be performed during the last
days of the month Tammuz, the days of mourning for
Tammuz, the officiating priest is instructed to offer certain
gifts to Ishtar, together with food offerings, associating
therewith the name of the patient. Invocations are then
addressed to Ishtar, Tammuz, and the Anunnaki, the gods
of the underworld. A bed is prepared for Tammuz, and
the sick man stands at the foot of the bed and covers his
face. The priest then strikes him seven times with a seven-
knotted cord (or reed). The ritual says that as soon as the
man has been struck by the priest he is changed, i.e. a
change of personality has been magically effected. The
continuation of the ritual shows what is meant by this, since
the priest goes on to say, 'Ishtar, thy beloved shall come
to thy side', and the sick man proceeds to enact the part of
Tammuz, striking himself and invoking Ishtar to save her
people. The priest then cuts off the hair of the sick man's
forehead, removes his girdle, and throws them, with food-
offerings, into the river. The patient is then to fast for three
days and go in sackcloth. This completes the ritual.

If we may accept Ebeling's interpretation of this ritual,
it is the magical re-enactment of the passion of Tammuz
by which the sufferer from the attack of the evil spirit is
delivered.

A number of similar examples from exorcism and
incantation-rituals might be cited, all suggesting that the
potency of the ritual lay in the re-enactment in symbolic

[1] E. Ebeling, op. cit., pp. 55 f.

form of some central element of the New Year ritual, in which the death or triumph of the god is involved. An example of another kind, but illustrating the same principle, is quoted by Mr. Gadd in *Myth and Ritual*,[1] and is fairly well known. It is a ritual for toothache, in which the efficacious spell pronounced by the priest consists of a portion of one of the various forms of the Creation story, and, as has been already pointed out, the significance of creation in Babylonian religion is ritual rather than cosmological. The power of the magical processes by which creation was originally effected is set in operation by the uttering of the spell for the cure of the toothache.

ii. *Omens*. The whole practice of the art of the *barû*-priest, or seer, while less involved in elaborate ritual actions than the operations of the *mašmašu* and *ašipu*-priests, rests upon the same presuppositions. Certain causes were believed to produce certain effects without fail, and it was also believed that the working of those causes was most clearly seen in the situations which the great central rituals depicted in their season. We have already seen that an important source of omens was found in the observance of the king's behaviour on the occasion of the New Year Festival, and it is interesting to note that the significance of many of the omens drawn from the appearance of the entrails and the liver is interpreted from events in the time of Sargon or Naram-Sin.

Many of the animals and birds from whose behaviour omens were drawn are symbols of gods and enter into the myth and ritual, hence their significance would come under the same explanation of general origin, and this holds good of the celestial bodies which were a most important source of omens.

It was only natural that in the course of its long history the practice of augury, comparatively simple at first, should proliferate into an immense and complicated system which it required years for a priest to master, and that many of

[1] Op. cit., p. 66.

its details should appear arbitrary and unrelated to any central principle.

It would be possible to go through the remaining classes of ritual, both public and private, and show that the same principle runs through them all, namely, the belief that it is possible to control the mysterious and seemingly arbitrary powers of nature, and that the secret of this control is to be found in certain original situations and events, symbolically depicted in the myths and re-enacted in the central rituals. In the New Year ritual, in particular, lay an immense reservoir of potency, both for good and ill, which could be tapped and controlled by the proper use of ritual, and in the proper use and due knowledge of the ritual lay the essence of Babylonian religion.

How far this principle may be discovered at work in the religion of Canaan, and whether its influence may be traced in the development of the religion of the Hebrews, are the questions to which we must turn our attention in the succeeding lectures.

PLATE I

(*a*) RITUAL SLAYING OF KING-GOD (*see p.* 11)

(*b*) THE GOD IN THE 'MOUNTAIN' (*see pp.* 11–12)
CUTTING DOWN OF TREE (*see p.* 14)

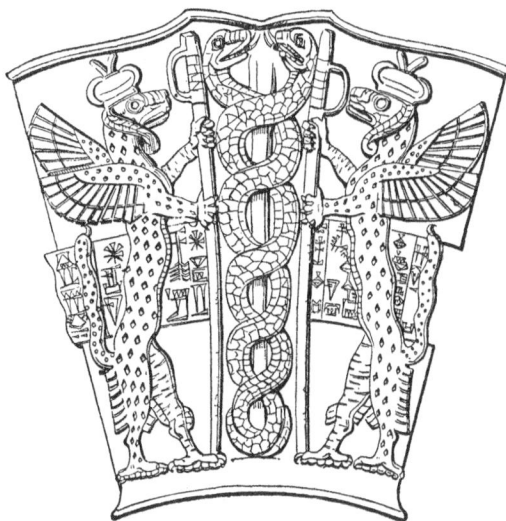

(*c*) ENTWINED SERPENTS (*see p.* 16)

PLATE II

(a) SLAYING OF THE SEVEN-HEADED HYDRA (see p. 14)

(b) SACRED MARRIAGE (see p. 16)

(c) RITUAL SLAYING OF KING-GOD (see p. 14)

PLATE III

(*a*) THE LAMAŠTU (*see p.* 20)

(*b*) THE GOD WITH STREAMS (*see p.* 39)

LECTURE II

THE task of attempting a description of the early religious system of Canaan is not an easy one. It somewhat resembles that of the palaeontologist who has to reconstruct the skeleton of an extinct mammal from a bone or two, and there is this at least in common between the two endeavours, that both are guided by the knowledge of an original pattern. It has been suggested in the previous lecture that the structure of the ritual system of the early religion of Mesopotamia may provide us with such a pattern, and it is hardly necessary, in the light of the results of modern archaeological discovery, to demonstrate the profound influence of Mesopotamian culture upon the surrounding and dependent countries.

Until a comparatively recent period our sources for the knowledge of early Canaanite religion were extremely scanty. They consisted mainly of vague accounts coming from late Greek historiographers and early Christian Fathers; of the very valuable information contained in the Old Testament, vitiated somewhat by the fact that it was not always contemporary, and suffered from the hostile attitude of the Hebrew writers who described it, since to them it appeared to be an utterly horrible and bestial system; and, finally, of the indirect evidence of the material remains of early Canaanite culture brought to light by archaeological excavation in Palestine.

To-day, however, we are in possession of a new and extremely valuable first-hand written source of information concerning the myth and ritual of an important centre of civilization in the north of Syria, belonging to the period practically contemporary with the Tell el-Amarna Letters, i.e. about the fourteenth century B.C. This material consists of a large number of tablets, written in a new form of alphabetic script, discovered in a chamber of a temple in the ancient trading centre of Ugarit, in the extreme north-west

corner of the Mediterranean coast, close to the modern
Latakia. The decipherment of this material, through the
labours of the late Hans Bauer, E. Dhorme, and C. Virolleaud, with the subsequent contributions of many distinguished Oriental scholars, has shown that the texts consist
of lists of gods, tables of offerings, and lexical tablets,
together with the largest and most important group of all,
namely, a collection, in poetic form, of early Canaanite
myths, unmistakably intended for ritual use.[1]

Apart from the evidence of the Ras Shamra tablets, to
which this lecture will be mainly devoted, there are three
main sources of evidence for the nature of the ritual practised by the inhabitants of Canaan before and during the
period of Hebrew settlement in the country. These will be
touched on briefly before we pass on to the Ras Shamra
material.

First there is the archaeological evidence. Apart from the
Ras Shamra tablets, the inscriptional evidence is meagre.
From the Zendjirli, Nerab, and Phoenician material col-
lected in the CIS and Lidzbarski, and in Cooke's *North
Semitic Inscriptions*, we gather some information about funerary ritual and the sacrificial system. But until the discovery
of the Ras Shamra material there was nothing to enable us
to gain a comprehensive picture of the ritual and its central
significance. Much more light has been gained from the
recent excavational activity in Palestine. The modern era
of excavation in Palestine may be said to have begun with
the systematic work done by Macalister at Gezer.[2] From
Gezer we learnt the general features of a great Canaanite
sanctuary, its rock altar, its masseboth, or sacred pillars, its
asherah, or sacred pole, and its underground chambers,
possibly for oracular responses. We also learnt of the existence of Egyptian funerary ritual at Gezer, which was only
to be expected from the history of the place. The picture

---

[1] A bibliography of the Ras Shamra material will be found in an
appendix.

[2] R. A. S. Macalister, *The Excavation of Gezer* (1912).

of Canaanite ritual at Gezer was supplemented and enlarged by the results of the scientific excavation of many other sites in Palestine. Vast numbers of Astarte figurines and amulets showed how widespread was the use of such charms for apotropaic or fertility purposes. The splendid work done by Mr. Crowfoot at Samaria, Mr. Alan Rowe at Bethshan, Professor Garstang at Jericho, and Mr. Starkey at Tell Duweir, the site of ancient Lachish, to mention only some of the most recent work, has supplemented and amplified the results of earlier workers; nor must the excellent work of Professor Albright and his collaborators in the American School of Oriental Research fail to receive its due meed of recognition in this connexion. Canaanite temples have been laid bare, examples of every kind of cult object have been recovered from their agelong burial, and the main external pattern of religious life has been reconstructed from the results of excavation.[1]

But on the whole it must be said that the result of this evidence, essential as it is to a complete picture of religious life in early Canaan, is mainly external, and does not give us an insight into the inner nature of the religion and into the dominant conceptions which underlay the ritual practices which are the core of all early religion. It is this unifying knowledge which, as we shall see, has been supplied for the first time in satisfying quantity by the new material from Ras Shamra.

The second source, of immense importance, is the information concerning Canaanite religion which is furnished by the writers of the Hebrew sacred books. It must, however, be pointed out that there are certain limitations to the use and value of this information. In the first place the only source for the state of Canaanite religion in the patriarchal period is the book of Genesis, and this book gives us only the faintest hints of what kind of religion the first Hebrew settlers found when they entered the land. We can discern

---

[1] Cf. especially H. G. May and R. M. Engberg, *Material Remains of the Megiddo Cult* (1935).

the existence of great Canaanite sanctuaries, such as Bethel and Shechem; we can infer the existence of the cults of local deities at sacred springs and groves; but all this only in shadowy outline. The editors of this book, which was probably the last book of the Pentateuch to receive its final form, were not concerned to preserve for posterity the exact knowledge of a religion which by their time had become little more than a vague memory, and which they could only regard as best buried in oblivion: they were interested solely in giving the final touches to a theodicy; to set forth the ancient traditions of their racial origins in such a light as to present the Hebrew people as from the first the object of the immutable purpose of their God.

The second limitation is that such accounts as we have of the relations between the Hebrews and the Canaanites during the period of conquest, if we may call it such, are almost entirely from the pen of prophetic writers who are hostile to the fundamental principle of Canaanite religion, as we shall see more clearly later on. The evidence of Hosea and Amos, and of the greater prophets, such as Isaiah and Jeremiah, shows that they were quite aware of the nature of the religion which the Hebrews had found living and active when they settled down in Palestine, and by which they had been more profoundly influenced than these writers would have cared to admit. Hence, on the one hand, we have a biased account of the practices of the Canaanites, which prevents us from understanding their significance for the people who practised them, and, on the other hand, the prophetic recasting of the national traditions has almost entirely obliterated the traces of the pre-prophetic religion of the Hebrews themselves. The result is a curious dualism, or dichotomy, in the history of Hebrew religion. We have an apparent protest against ritual in every form, including all sacrifices and seasonal festivals, reaching its climax in Jeremiah's rejection of the very core of the ritual system of Hebrew religion, the Temple at Jerusalem, and the ancient palladium of the national history, the ark of Jahweh. Against this we have the activities of the priestly class in preserving the traditions of the ritual system connected with the Temple, and their success in restoring a full Temple service after the Exile, which only perished with the destruction of the Temple itself in A.D. 70.

Hence our direct information from Hebrew sources concerning Canaanite ritual is mainly limited to the various ritual prohibitions in the different layers of Pentateuchal legislation, and to occasional references in the historical parts of the Old Testament to such practices as human sacrifice, or such scenes as are described in the vivid account of the frenzied behaviour of the Priests of the Tyrian Baal on Carmel.

But in recent years much indirect information has been gained from the study of the poetic parts of the Old Testament, and in spite of a certain natural conservative reluctance, it is being gradually admitted that a great deal of the liturgical material in the Psalms throws light on the ritual of the pre-prophetic religion of the Hebrews, and inferentially on the kindred ritual of their Canaanite neighbours. But this will be discussed more fully in the last lecture, as also will the significance of the Hebrew seasonal festivals, and their relation to Canaanite agricultural rituals. It would be possible to go through all the ritual prohibitions in the Pentateuch, even apparently trivial ones, and to show that they have connexions with those elements in the central conceptions of Canaanite and Mesopotamian religion which were most repugnant to the main tendency of Hebrew religion. It may also be added that the fact that prohibition of such practices was necessary shows that they existed, not only among the Canaanites, but among the Hebrews at the time of the promulgation of such laws.[1] It may suffice here to point out that not only do the prohibitions provide evidence for whole groups of customs connected with the central rites of Canaanite and Mesopotamian religion, but

[1] See *Myth and Ritual*, pp. 70 ff.

also a number of ancient customs which assume the form of injunctions in the Pentateuchal legislation similarly represent vestigial remains of similar rites.

The third source of information for early Canaanite ritual is found in late Greek writers such as Philo of Byblus, Lucian, Diodorus, Damasius, and others. Of these the most important is Philo of Byblus, since he is the only writer who attempts to do for Canaanite traditions what Berossus did for early Babylonian traditions. Unfortunately his work is only preserved in fragments quoted by Eusebius in his *Praeparatio Evangelica*. Considering how far Philo was removed from his source, it is surprising how closely the outlines of his description correspond to the general outline of the Ras Shamra myth.

The information given by Lucian and other writers concerning the late forms of the Adonis myth and ritual is only useful for our purpose as bearing witness to the continuity of the Tammuz-Adonis tradition in Palestine to a very late date.

But for the early form of that cult in Canaan we shall have to depend entirely on the evidence of the Ras Shamra tablets in comparison with the new evidence for the nature of the early Mesopotamian cult of Tammuz recently published.

We shall therefore turn now to the most important part of the evidence for the nature of early Canaanite religion, its pantheon and its ritual, namely, the Ras Shamra tablets.

The Ras Shamra Tablets. The French excavations at Minet el-beida and Ras Shamra, directed by M. Claude Schaeffer, were begun in the spring of 1929, as the result of the discovery, made by a peasant while ploughing his field, of the covering stone of a vaulted sepulchral chamber. Minet el-beida, the site of the discovery, is a small natural harbour, about eight miles north of Latakia. Excavations were carried on at Minet el-beida and at the neighbouring tell of Ras Shamra. It was found that the latter was the site of an ancient city, which has since been identified as

Ugarit, mentioned both in the Tell el-Amarna Letters and in contemporary Assyrian sources.[1]

The site was found to be rich in remains of a civilization which goes back to the twelfth dynasty, and probably to prehistoric times. As might have been expected from its situation, the site showed a very interesting mingling of many cultures, Aegean, Hittite, Hurrian, Mesopotamian, Egyptian, and Canaanite.

A large number of inscribed tablets were found in what has been called by the discoverers the library of the temple. Many of these were written in a script which appeared at first sight to be cuneiform, but which proved on examination to be a new form of alphabetic script; and the language was revealed as a West-Semitic dialect, closely akin to Hebrew and so-called Phoenician, but not hitherto met with in inscriptions.

The interest attaching to a new form of script and language was quickly surpassed by the extraordinary nature of the contents of the tablets. They were found to contain, in poetic form and diction, a series of episodes reflecting the mythology of early Canaanite religion. The ritual nature of the material was very evident. M. C. Virolleaud has been engaged for several years in the decipherment and translation of the texts, and while it will be many years before the numerous philological and cultural problems raised by this new material can be solved, it is at least possible to offer some provisional results concerning the gods, myths, and ritual of early Canaanite religion as disclosed in these tablets.

Apart from various miscellaneous tablets, all of which have contributed something to the knowledge of cultural conditions at Ugarit, the main body of mythological texts so far published by M. Virolleaud appear to fall into the following groups, named and numbered by him according

[1] The name of Ugarit also occurs in a recently deciphered text found in 1936 in the course of M. Parrot's excavation of Mari. See *Syria*, xviii. 1, p. 74, n. 1 (1937).

to their subject-matter and the order in which they hap-
pened to be translated. As the successive portions were
published, it became clear that some rearrangement of
their order would be necessary:

(a) I AB: The Fight between Mot, the son of the Gods,
    and Aleyan-Baal, the son of Baal.
(b) II AB: A new Song of the Poem of Aleyan-Baal.
(c) SS: The Birth of the Beautiful and Gracious Gods.
(d) I AB: A New Fragment of the Poem of Mot and
    Aleyan-Baal. This contained the 28 lines missing
    from the beginning of (a) and the 19 lines from
    the end. These lines are marked with an asterisk
    in M. Virolleaud's edition in *Syria* to distinguish
    them from the lines already numbered in (a).
(e) I*AB: The Death of Baal, a text which precedes (a).
(f) III AB, A: The Revolt of Košer against Baal.

Hence the rearranged order of the texts, according to
M. Virolleaud, is now, (e), (d, ll. 1–28), (a), (d, ll. 38–57),
(b) and (f); the relation of (c) to the poem of Aleyan-Baal
is not determined, nor is the relation of II AB to I AB
certain.

The general summary of the contents of the texts in their
rearranged order is as follows:

In the opening lines of (e), which apparently are the
continuation of a previous discourse, possibly belonging to
the end of II AB (so Virolleaud, *Syria*, xv, p. 308), Baal
gives instructions to his messenger, Gepen-Ugar, to slay
Leviathan, the swift serpent, and the crooked dragon with
seven heads, and to obtain a certain magical object. He is
then to bear a message to Mot, the Lord of the lower
world, seeking reconciliation. Gepen-Ugar seems to have
failed in the task appointed to him, but brings back a
message from Mot inviting Baal to a banquet in the nether
world which he has prepared. Baal replies by repeating
his orders to Gepen-Ugar to slay the two serpents. Then,
after a break in the text, the disappearance of Baal is described, and the withering of vegetation. Aleyan-Baal

laments and sends a message to the Yošeb-elim asking for
his intercession, and a message to Mot reproaching him.
Then follows a very broken passage which appears to
describe some kind of banquet, possibly in the underworld.
Another fragmentary passage contains references to what
may be a funerary feast to which the spirits of the underworld are summoned. Then follow instructions, either from
Baal, speaking perhaps from the underworld, or from some
deity who has been mentioned in the preceding broken
lines, to Aleyan-Baal, to bring his attributes, clouds, winds,
and rain, and his attendants, among whom Virolleaud
finds mention of eight boars, and repair to the underworld,
thus announcing his approaching death. The next scene
appears to describe, in symbolic form, a fertility rite, a
sacred marriage. Aleyan-Baal loves a heifer and a child
is born named Mes or Mos, a name which is not yet
explained. Then follows the announcement of the death
of Aleyan-Baal, and the description of the mourning of
Ltpn-Eldpd, the funeral rites of Aleyan-Baal, and the
search for Baal himself, who is also declared to be dead,
by Ltpn-Eldpd and Anat. The text closes with the burial
of Baal by Anat.

The next fragment (d) contains the first 28 lines of (a),
Virolleaud's I AB. Here we have apparently the continuation of (e), and the description of the funeral rites performed by Anat for Baal, and then, with the assistance
of Šapaš, for Aleyan-Baal. The sacrifices are unusual: 70
wild-oxen, 70 bulls, 70 sheep, 70 stags, 70 wild-goats, and
70 asses. The continuation, in (a), describes the search of
Anat for Aleyan-Baal, and the rejoicing of Asherat. El
asks Asherat that a substitute-king for Aleyan-Baal may
be appointed from among her sons. Ltpn-Eldpd advises
that Ashtar-Arif be made king; the latter is accordingly
enthroned on the heights of Zaphon, the mount of the
north, the ancient abode of Aleyan-Baal. Anat continues
her search for her brother, Aleyan-Baal, and ultimately
comes to Mot and demands her brother. Then follows

a curious scene in which Anat splits Mot with the *harpé*, or ritual sickle, winnows him, roasts him, grinds him, sows him, and gives him to the birds to eat. After the death of Mot, Ltpn-Eldpd hears in a dream that Aleyan-Baal is alive, and that fertility is about to return. He rejoices and announces the news to Anat. But although Aleyan-Baal lives, he is not yet found, and the search continues, with the assistance of Šapaš. Then we have, in apparent incon-sistency with the death of Mot, already described, an account of the victory of Baal over Mot and his followers, and a threat to Aleyan-Baal from Mot that after seven years he will undergo the fate which Mot himself is described as having undergone at the hands of Anat. Aleyan-Baal returns and sits on the throne of Baal; Šapaš announces the doom of Mot, and his forsaking by his father, the Bull-El. Mot goes down to the underworld and Aleyan-Baal is enthroned. The last lines of this text and the colophon are contained in (*d*). They consist of an invocation to Šapaš in her character of guardian of the spirits of the dead, and a ritual casting of two objects, whose names are uncertain, into the sea by Košer-u-Ḥasis. These two fragments give both the superscription of the whole text, 'To Baal', and the colophon with the name of the scribe, and that of the contemporary king of Ugarit, Neqmed, a name which is found again in the Kirkuk Tablets. The latter would, however, appear to be earlier in date than our texts.

Hence (*e*), (*d*), and (*a*) together appear to present a complete ritual text with remarkable affinities to the Tammuz myth and ritual. We shall return to the discus-sion of the Tammuz parallels later.

The remaining texts, although they deal with the same personages in the main, and are also clearly ritual texts, are not necessaıily connected with the ritual contained in the texts already described.

The first of these, (*b*), Virolleaud's II AB, is the longest of the texts so far published, and the most obscure, although it contains a great deal of most valuable material. It has also received the most attention from scholars hitherto. The following is a summary of its contents:

The beginning of the tablet being broken, the first intelligible lines mention various dwellings of the different gods, and a declaration that Baal has no house like the other gods. Hiyan, the artificer god, then appears and makes objects, possibly figurines or images of bulls, out of gold and silver. A golden throne is made and set up, and offerings and libations prescribed, possibly to El. Then Anat appears on the scene, and, according to Virolleaud, attacks Mot with the help of Aleyan-Baal and discomfits him. Here there is considerable disagreement among the scholars who have attempted the interpretation of this passage. Dussaud, Albright and Barton, although differing in details, agree in finding here a description of certain magical actions performed by Anat or Asherat or both, possibly in preparation for the building of the house for Baal. The next episode is also too uncertain to describe, as the widely varying versions show; it probably contains a description of the part played by Aleyan-Baal in the arrangements for the building and the preparatory sacrifices. The next episode is clearer and describes a procession of the goddess Asherat-yam, mounted on a richly decked foal, led by the gods Qadesh and Amurru, to the field of El, where she entreats El to allow a house to be built for Baal. Then either El, or perhaps Ltpn-Eldpd as his representative, invites Asherat to a banquet, and announces a sacred marriage between the Bull-El and the goddess. Ltpn-Eldpd promises to undertake the building of the temple, and is promised by Asherat as a reward the refreshing rain of heaven. Asherat goes on to make arrangements for pilgrimages and the provision of materials and money for the building. Provisions are also to be made from animals slain in the chase for the builder Košer-u-Ḥasis, who is instructed by Aleyan-Baal to proceed with the work. Then occurs a curious dispute between the

F

builder and Aleyan-Baal as to whether the inner shrine shall be furnished with a window or not. How the dispute is finally settled appears from a later reference, Košer-u-Ḥasis is satisfied and the work proceeds. Cedars are brought from Lebanon, a point which Dussaud urges in support of the Phoenician origin of these poems. Then follows a great sacrificial ritual and dedicatory feast in which Aleyan-Baal and the seventy sons of Asherat participate, and the rite of the sacred marriage seems to form part of the dedicatory ritual. Baal assumes his divine and royal insignia and enters his new abode.[1] The windows of the temple are then opened, evidently as a rain charm or ritual. Finally, Baal proclaims his triumph over Mot, assumes responsibility for fertility and prosperity, and sends messengers to Mot assigning to him his place in the underworld, and as ruler over the unwatered plains, while to Aleyan-Baal belong the lands watered by the rain of heaven. Baal orders the conflict between Aleyan-Baal and Mot to cease.

It is clear that this very difficult text describes a dedicatory ritual and its associated myth. It presents interesting parallels, both with the dedication of Solomon's temple and with the dedicatory rites of Hanukkah. To these points we shall return later.

The two texts which remain to be described are (ƒ), Virolleaud's III AB, A, described by him as *The Revolt of Košer against Baal*, and (c), Virolleaud's SS, entitled *The Birth of the Beautiful and Gracious Gods*. These also are ritual texts, embodying myths, but their connexion with the preceding texts is not clear.

The contents of the latter are as follows:

The text begins with an invocation to the gods described as gracious and fair, whose birth is described subsequently. Then follows a series of short rituals, with invocations and what appear to be rubrics containing instructions for the officiants.

---

[1] Cf. R. Dussaud, RHR, cxi. 29.

1. The first is a symbolic pruning of vines, which may indicate the breaking of Mot's rule of barrenness and desolation.

2. The second is the rite, forbidden in the Book of the Covenant, of seething a kid in milk. Many interpreters, following Frazer, explain this as a milk-charm, but later evidence of the presence of this rite in the Orphic Mysteries suggests that it had originally a more esoteric significance than a milk-charm.

3. The third is an interesting piece of ritual in which priests go to the sea and pour ladlefuls of water into basins which are then borne into the temple by El, probably impersonated by the king or the high-priest. El sends down the early rain, that is, the autumn rain, the Hebrew *yoreh*.

4. The fourth act is the flaying and roasting of a bird, symbolizing Mot. This may be compared with the slaying of the bird which is the symbol of a god on the seals from Tell Asmar.[1]

5. The fifth is the important and frequently occurring ritual of the sacred marriage, here apparently carried out by the temple priests with the hierodules.

6. This is followed by the announcement of the tidings to El that the result of the previous ritual has been the birth of seven gods, the Gracious and Beautiful Gods of Virolleaud's title. The seventh is Shalem, who is destined to rebuild Ashdod.

7. The last describes the ritual wanderings in the wilderness of a goddess, possibly Asherat, and the hierodules. The wilderness is the wilderness of Kadesh.

While it is possible that the text is a collection of separate rituals or incantations, for use on various occasions, it is more probable, from the recurrence of Mot and other elements throughout the text, that it represents a complete ritual possibly for use at an autumn festival. The apparent connexion with the south of Palestine, if we may accept the

[1] Cf. H. Frankfort, *Iraq*, i. 1. p. 28 and n. 1.

mention of the Arabim, Kadesh, and Ashdod as correctly read, raises interesting possibilities concerning the origin of these texts.

The last of the longer texts hitherto published that calls for description is (*f*), the so-called revolt of Košer against Baal. The text opens with a violent storm which breaks the forest trees. According to Dussaud's reading,[1] based on an ingenious use of the metrical principles of the poetry of Ras Shamra, the action begins with the transmission of the orders of Baal by the goddess Asherat to the Baalim, or lesser deities attendant on Baal, to attack the throne of Aleyan-Baal, here called the Zebul-yam, or ruler of the sea. Possibly an earlier portion of the tablet, whose beginning is mutilated, would explain the reason of these orders, since, in the other texts which we have described, Aleyan-Baal is always on the side of his father, Baal. Then Košer-u-Ḥasis, whom we have already heard of as the builder of the temple of Baal, stirs up Aleyan-Baal to attack the Baalim and seize the supreme power. The scene represents Aleyan-Baal in his chariot, which is guided by Košer-u-Ḥasis, driving the horses of the sea against the chariot of Baal, guided by Bod-Baal. The fight is spiritedly described, and has many interesting echoes of poetic passages in the Old Testament. The issue of the contest is the victory and the capture of Aleyan-Baal, with the consequent calming of the agitated waters. Aleyan attempts to excuse himself for his revolt against his father by saying that he was attacked by the Baalim, who were seeking to kill the sea. Here unfortunately the text breaks off.

While this text presents us with a very definite myth, it is less easy than in the case of the previous texts to discover

---

[1] R. Dussaud, 'Les Éléments déchaînés' in *Syria*, xvi. 11. It should, however, be remarked that there is a considerable divergence of opinion among the various scholars who have attempted an interpretation of this poem. For other views cf. W. F. Albright in JPOS, xvi. 17 ff. (1936); J. A. Montgomery, JAOS, lv. 3, pp. 268 ff. (1935); T. H. Gaster, *Iraq*, iv. 1, pp. 21 ff. (1937).

the nature of the ritual, if there is one, which it implies. The myth falls into line with that of the conquest of Tiamat by Marduk, and of the subjugation of the waters by Jahweh, so often the subject of Hebrew poetry,[1] and the fact that these myths implied a definite ritual is certain in the case of Babylonian religion, though it has yet to be discussed for Hebrew religion. Hence there is a presupposition in favour of a connexion between this myth of Ugarit and some ritual, possibly, as Mr. T. H. Gaster suggests, belonging to the season of the winter rains, storms, and floods.

Our survey would not be complete without mention of certain passages in some of the shorter texts from Ras Shamra which have an important bearing on the question of the nature of Canaanite ritual. Some of these texts were among the first to be deciphered and published, and it was inevitable that mistakes should have been made in translating and interpreting them. But the publication of the longer texts, due to the infinite labour and skill of M. Virolleaud, has thrown so much light that we can now approach them with more confidence.

The earliest ritual text to be published was a list of gods and the offerings assigned to them, translated by E. Dhorme.[2] This is not only of importance as showing a fully developed ritual organization of gods, temples, personnel, and sacrifices, at the time to which these texts belong, but also as throwing valuable light on the whole question of the nature of sacrifice in Canaan. We shall refer to this text later.

Another of these earlier texts contains interesting evidence of the nature of the ritual connected with the right of asylum, and the oath.

But the most important evidence coming from these shorter texts is that of the presence of Egyptian elements in the ritual of Ugarit. We have a ritual in which Asherat, i.e. Astarte-Hathor, introduces Horus into the temple, and

---

[1] Cf. Ps. xciii and Hab. iii.
[2] *Revue biblique*, 1931, pp. 32–56.

in which the king plays an important part; a ritual which
Egyptian parallels suggest must have been connected
with the sacred marriage. A text published by Mr. T. H.
Gaster gives further evidence as to the presence of Horus
elements in the ritual of Ugarit.[1]

We must now attempt an estimate of the nature of the
evidence afforded by these texts as to the various types of
ritual which formed part of the religious life of an important city in northern Syria towards the end of the second
millennium B.C.

It should also be observed, since the point is of great
importance for the question of the relation of the religion
of Ugarit to that of the early Hebrews, that both linguistic
evidences and topographical references in the texts suggest
a connexion with southern Palestine, as also does the discovery of a tablet at Bethshemesh written in the Ras Shamra
alphabetic script.[2]

In this lecture we shall confine ourselves mainly to estab-
lishing the parallels between the ritual practices of Ugarit
and the general character of Mesopotamian ritual, leaving
the question of parallels with early Hebrew ritual to the
last lecture of this series.

First of all, it is very clear that one of the most important
elements in Mesopotamian ritual, the conception of the
dying and rising god, is also characteristic of the myth and
ritual of Ugarit. But while in the New Year ritual in its
later form in Babylon the agricultural aspect of the ritual
has receded into the background, this aspect remains
prominent in the Ugarit myth and ritual. In this respect
the form of the Canaanite ritual is much more akin to the
earlier Tammuz ritual in Mesopotamia. We find that
the death of Baal and Aleyan-Baal and their descent into the
underworld is connected with drought and the withering
of all vegetation, a feature which has disappeared from the
late Babylonian form of the Akitu-Festival, but which recurs

---

[1] *Egyptian Religion*, iii. 2.
See BASOR, lii. 3 ff. (1933).

over and over again in the Tammuz liturgies. An interesting parallel with the Babylonian form of the myth is that neither in the Canaanite myth, as far as our knowledge goes at present, nor in the Babylonian myth, is the manner of the death of the god, which must have formed part of the ritual, described. In both there is the trace of the possible defeat and death of the god at the hands of an opponent, symbolized by some dragon or other bestial form. Two points of resemblance are to be noted in this connexion; in the first Ras Shamra text described above we find a seven-headed dragon as one of the opponents of Baal, to which there is a parallel in the seven-headed dragon or hydra represented on the seal from Tell Asmar. Secondly, the pig which appears to be the substitute for the god in KAT 9555 finds a parallel in the eight boars, if we may accept this rendering of *ḫnzrm*, which are associated with Aleyan-Baal, and with the later tradition of the slaying of Adonis by a boar.

Then the search and mourning for the dead god by his sister and consort is common to both the Canaanite and the Mesopotamian Tammuz and Marduk rituals. An interesting feature of this part of the Ras Shamra texts is that certain ritual vessels play a part in the search for the dead god in the underworld, and seem to be connected with the need for the streams needed for irrigation. There is clearly a close connexion between the dead god and these vessels. In her book *The Flowing Vase and the God with Streams* Mrs. Van Buren has shown the constant connexion, on seals and other pictorial representations, of a vase from which water is flowing, with a divine figure, usually Ningiszida, who is frequently equated with Tammuz in the liturgies.

Another element which has receded into the background in the Babylonian New Year ritual, but which remains prominent in the Ras Shamra texts, is the significance of the underworld and its ruler. We have rites intended to propitiate the dwellers in the underworld, and Mot prepares a banquet in the underworld to which he invites Baal.

This underworld aspect of the cult is prominent in the Tammuz liturgies.

The closest parallel in the Ras Shamra texts to the slaying of Tiamat by Marduk, which leads up to the Creation and the fixing of destinies, is the symbolic treatment of Mot by Anat, but here the agricultural significance of the ritual remains foremost. In the first text discussed Baal declares that the consequence of the victory over the dragons would be the acquisition of a certain magical object whose name at present is of unascertained meaning, but the word by which it is designated, *trp*, suggests a connexion with the name of the magical *teraphim*, connected with divination in early Hebrew religion. A tentative comparison may be suggested with the magical tablets of destiny which play such an important part in various Babylonian myths, and upon the possession of which the control of magical powers seems to depend.

One more point in connexion with the theme of the dying and rising god in these texts calls for remark. It is that they present the conception of a regular alternation in the possession of power by Aleyan-Baal and his father on the one hand, and Mot on the other.[1] There is a suggestion of a period of seven years as the duration of the power of each, recalling the seven years of plenty succeeded by seven years of famine familiar to us from Pharaoh's dream in Genesis. But there is also the suggestion that the myth and its associated ritual represent the two periods of the agricultural year in Canaan, the period of summer heat and drought, when vegetation withers, and Mot rules, and the period of the rains, the revival of vegetation and the filling of the streams, symbolized by the resurrection of Aleyan-Baal and his rule over the land. Probably this alternation was much more marked in the Tammuz myth and ritual in Mesopotamia, as the Tammuz liturgies suggest, but is overlaid in the later Babylonian

[1] Cf. the discussion of this point in *Culture and Conscience*, W. C. Graham and H. G. May, pp. 129 ff. (1936).

form of the New Year ritual by the more urban characteristics of the festival, as Pallis maintains.

Enough has been said to show how large a place in
early Canaanite ritual was occupied by the central idea
of the dying and rising god.

When we turn to the second main feature of the Mesopotamian ritual, the sacred marriage, we find that this
rite is exceedingly prominent in our texts. It occurs in the
first group of texts in the form of a marriage between Aleyan-
Baal and a cow, which results in the birth of a child named
Mes or Mos. This episode in the ritual has been connected
with the prohibition of what has been called 'bestiality' in
Lev. xviii. 23, xx. 15; but it is possible that the cult action
here described is purely symbolic. In the dedication ritual
the celebrations at the dedication of Baal's temple include
a sacred marriage; while the climax of the group of rituals
in the text entitled *The Birth of the Beautiful and Gracious
Gods* is the celebration in the temple of a sacred marriage
between the priests of El and the temple hierodules, resulting
in the birth of the seven gods. It is possible that further
texts will throw light on the nature of these gods, and that
they will prove to be a group of lesser deities or demi-gods
with compound names, such as Shalem-u-Škhar, Košer-u-
Ḥasis, possessing special attributes of wisdom or magical
knowledge, like the Cabeiri.

Hence, our evidence shows that the sacred marriage was
an important element in early Canaanite ritual, and that
it was connected, as in the early Mesopotamian ritual, with
the promotion of fertility. But it was not primarily connected
with a New Year ritual, being found in connexion with
various types and occasions of ritual, and we saw that the
same was true of the place of this ceremony in Mesopotamian
ritual.

It has been already suggested that the long text called
II AB by Virolleaud seemed to present the characteristics
of a dedication ritual, and while it bristles with difficulties,
it raises several interesting points. The reappearance of the

ritual combat between Anat and Mot suggests that this ritual did form part of the New Year ceremonies, and that the building of a temple for Baal formed a climax to the episodes of the festival in the same way as the Babylonian Creation Epic represents the building of a temple for Marduk by the other gods as the reward for his victory over Tiamat.[1] A similar parallel is afforded by the banquet which follows the completion of the building, and we may also compare the enthronement of Enlil in the chapel of Ninlil in Nippur by the fifty gods and the seven gods who fixed the destinies. It is possible that the late Jewish festival of Hanukkah, the dedication of the restored temple in the Maccabean era, contained ritual elements which go back to very early tradition. We do not know the exact details of the dedication of Solomon's temple, but the water-rite which formed part of the Sukkah ritual[2] may well go back to the ritual implied in our text when Baal opens the window of the new temple and causes the streams to flow and the rains to descend. If the passage is correctly interpreted which seems to describe the lighting of fires in the new temple, we may have another parallel to the ritual lighting of lamps in the Hanukkah.[3]

A careful examination of the part played by the rather enigmatic figure of Ltpn-Eldpd, the son of Bull-El, in this text, gives ground for the suggestion that we have here the part played by the king in the ritual. The name may prove to be, like Meskalamdug in the Ur ritual, a title borne by the individual who took this part both in the dedication ritual, and who also appears in the ritual of the death of Baal as participating in the search for Baal and Aleyan-Baal together with Anat. It may also be the name of an early king of Ugarit. But the functions and activities of

---

[1] See *The Epic of Creation* (ed. Langdon), pp. 172–5.

[2] *Sukkah*, iv. 9–v. 1. For the connexion between Sukkah and Hanukkah see O. S. Rankin, *The Origins of the Festival of Hanukkah*, pp. 274–5 (1930).

[3] O. S. Rankin, op. cit., c. 3.

Ltpn-Eldpd seem to be rather those of a human actor in the cult drama than those of a god. Ltpn-Eldpd receives in a dream the revelation of the resurrection of Aleyan-Baal; it is he who undertakes the responsibility of providing for the building of the temple and the organization of its cult.

We have already discussed some of the features of the third text, *The Birth of the Beautiful and Gracious Gods*, but there are a few additional points which call for notice. The ritual, or rather the group of rituals, begins with the ceremonial pruning of the vines, and a cult commentary is added to say that this action represents the slaying of Mot. It emphasizes the predominantly agricultural character of these Canaanite rituals. Then we have the magical ritual already referred to, namely, the boiling of a kid in milk, which is forbidden in the Book of the Covenant. While this may have come to be regarded in the course of time simply as a milk-charm, the general symbolic character of all these rituals would suggest rather that we have here a piece of ritual which symbolizes the death and resurrection of Aleyan-Baal. This conjecture is supported by the place of the kid in Babylonian substitution rituals.

It may also be added that it is this group of rituals which possesses most markedly a south Palestinian colouring, and it is noteworthy that some of the most striking parallels with Hebrew ritual tradition occur in this group.

Two points call for notice in the last text, the so-called *Revolt of Košer against Baal*. First, the theme is that of a contest between Baal and the powers of the sea, in which Baal is victorious. We shall see later that there are striking echoes of this conflict in Hebrew poetic literature, but it may be remarked here that among maritime peoples there is manifest a tendency to develop some type of ritual which represents the same attempt to acquire control of the forces of the sea that we find expressed in the attempt to control the powers of nature connected with reproduction and fertility. One of the elements in the myth of Marduk and

Tiamat may have been the attempt to control the forces of the river, which meant so much for Mesopotamian civilization, and among a seafaring people one form which this myth and its connected ritual may have taken might have been a ritual representing the conquest of the unruly waters by the god.

The second point is that we seem to have in this text the myth of the rebellion of an honoured and important deity against a superior deity with whom he stands in close relation, a rebellion which fails. Moreover, the rebellion is instigated by a god or demi-god distinguished by his wisdom. It is tempting to see in this myth the elements which underlie both the Hebrew myth of the fall of the Son of the Morning, and Ezekiel's description of the fall of the Prince of Tyre.

Thus we see from these extraordinarily interesting texts, in spite of the many unsolved problems which they present, clear evidence of the general character of early Canaanite ritual, and of the close relation which it bears to the type of ritual which we have already found occupying the central place in the early religion of Mesopotamia. In the last lecture we shall attempt to relate what we know of early Hebrew ritual and its later developments to both Canaanite and Mesopotamian ritual.

IT may seem both impertinent and a work of superero-
gation to attempt to garner sheaves in a field which has
already been so abundantly laboured in by eminent scholars
of the past and present generations. But the discovery in
recent years of much fresh light on the whole field of the
early religion of the ancient East invites an attempt to set
the familiar material of Hebrew ritual in a new perspective.
In the two previous lectures we have taken a rapid survey
of the general character of early Mesopotamian and Canaanite ritual, and of their relation to one another. It remains
to make a similar survey of Hebrew ritual and to discover
what is its relation to the religion which formed the cultural
environment of the Hebrews during the period of their settlement in Canaan.

The most difficult problem in dealing with the evidence
for the nature of Hebrew ritual is that the definitely ritual
parts of the Old Testament in their present form are all
later than the great prophetic movement which, from the
eighth century onwards, produced a cleavage between the
early pre-prophetic religion of Israel and the religion which
is reflected in the present form of the Pentateuch and in the
prophetic books.

It is now generally recognized that even the late parts
of the Pentateuch preserve much early material, and it is
legitimate to use evidence from the Deuteronomic and
Priestly legislation relating to the ritual, with due precau-
tion, as some indication of the forms of ritual which existed
in the pre-prophetic period. We have also valuable material
from the early historical books, Judges and 1 Samuel, and
in the early legislation, such as the collection of ritual
prescriptions contained in what is called the Book of the
Covenant. Similarly, the prohibitions in this and later
legislation, together with the denunciations of current
practices by the prophets, help us to gain some idea of the

state of early Hebrew ritual. Indirect evidence from later survivals, preserved in the Talmudic literature and in the Apocryphal books, may add some details to the picture, and recent studies in the liturgical use of the LXX show that valuable evidence for our purpose may be obtained from this source. Lastly, there is the indirect, but extremely important, evidence of the liturgical elements in the Psalter. Here recent researches have shown the possibility that the liturgical material was originally intended for use in the seasonal festivals and other ritual occasions in the pre-prophetic stage of Hebrew religion.

Hence, in our examination of the various types of ritual of which we have an account in the Old Testament, we shall have two main objects before us. First, to distinguish the earlier from the later forms of each type of ritual, and secondly, to discover, if possible, their relation to the ritual system which, as we have seen, prevailed in the Near East when the Hebrews were developing their own religion and culture.

1. Seasonal Rituals.

The earliest evidence for this class of ritual is found in the prescriptions of the Book of the Covenant. These ordinances exist in two parallel versions, that of E in Exod. xxiii. 14–19 and xxii. 29–30, and the J version in Exod. xxxiv. 18–26. Later elaborations of these seasonal festivals are found in the Deuteronomic Code, Deut. xvi. 1–17, and in the Priestly Code, Exod. xii. 1–20; Lev. xxiii; Num. ix. 1–14; xxviii and xxix. There are also historical, or quasi-historical allusions to occasions on which these seasonal festivals were held, in the historical books, and references in the prophetic literature to the existence of such festivals at the time of the activity of the various prophets. We will deal first of all with the evidence of the Book of the Covenant.

There are three seasonal feasts prescribed for the Hebrew in the Book of the Covenant, the Feast of Maṣṣoth, or Unleavened Bread; the Feast of Weeks, or Pentecost; and

the Feast of Ingathering, later known as the Feast of Tabernacles.

These are all agricultural festivals, and follow the course
of the farmer's year. The first of these, the Feast of Unleavened Bread, was held in the month Abib, the Babylonian Nisan, the beginning of the spring. From the form
of the prescription in the Priestly Code in Exod. xii we learn
that at some period in the development of Hebrew religion
the Feast of Unleavened Bread came to include other
elements beside the ritual eating of unleavened cakes, and
in the form of the Passover became a New Year Festival.
This feast raises several difficult problems, and must be
examined with some care.

The Book of the Covenant only tells us when the feast
was to be kept, and gives no details as to its ritual, save that
we may legitimately infer that the ritual sacrifice of the
firstborn was connected with the New Year Festival. Hence
we have to depend upon the late source in Exod. xii and
xiii for an account of the ritual elements in the feast, and
can only hazard an estimate of the period when the feast
was celebrated in this form from the internal evidence. It
need hardly be said that we cannot take the account of the
celebration in Exod. xii and xiii as historical, in the strict
sense. It is rather an example of the process which we find
abundantly illustrated in the history of the growth of the
Jewish festival calendar, by which ancient festivals whose
origins were lost in obscurity became attached to historical
events, or events which were regarded as historical in
Hebrew tradition. The first pre-exilic legislation which
associates the Passover with the tradition of the Exodus is
in Deuteronomy, if we may assume a pre-exilic date for the
passage, and the account of the first Passover observed in
the monarchical period, in the reign of Josiah (1 Kings
xxiii. 21–3), implies that the feast had not been kept, at
least with the proper rites, since the time of the judges.

But we may at least assume that the connexion in the
Priestly tradition of this feast with the event which was

regarded as the beginning of national history, points to its existence at a very early date. An examination of its details may help to confirm this assumption. The ritual details are as follows:

(a) The killing of a ritually perfect victim, a lamb or a kid, which has been held in readiness until the night of the full moon.

(b) The eating of the roast flesh of the victim, with unleavened bread and bitter herbs.

(c) The smearing of the blood of the victim upon the side-posts and lintels of the doors of the houses.

(d) It is forbidden for any one to leave the house until the morning.

(e) Nothing may be left over of the feast, and any remains must be burnt in the morning.

(f) A sacrifice of the firstborn is prescribed as part of the ritual. It is possible to deduce from Exod. xxii. 29 that this was originally a human sacrifice, although in the J version of the prescription, in Exod. xxxvi. 20, a substitute is permitted.

(g) The feast continues for seven days with the eating of unleavened bread.

If we remove from our minds the associations of the Passover with a particular event, it is easier to estimate its ritual implications. It is first of all a New Year Feast. It is a spring festival, whose preparations begin on the 10th of Abib (i.e. Nisan) and last until the 21st, eleven days in all, as in the Babylonian Akitu Festival.[1] Its central point is reached on the night of the 14th, the full moon. On this night the Destroyer is abroad; it is dangerous for any one to be outside the house during the night, and special apotropaic measures are taken to secure the houses from the invasion of the Destroyer.[2] We have already seen the constant use of the kid and the lamb in Babylonian apotropaic

[1] Cf. S. A. Pallis, *The Babylonian Akitu Festival*, pp. 120–31 (1926).
[2] Cf. N. Nicolsky, *Spüren Magischer Formeln in den Psalmen*, p. 9, n. 6 (1927).

ritual, both as a substitute and as a symbol of the god. Hence we may suggest that the ritual eating of the flesh of the victim was only one of the ways, of which we have various examples in Mesopotamian ritual, of substitution, of the identification of the interested person with the god as a means of deliverance from the attack of a hostile power. For instance, we have an example[1] in Babylonian incantation rituals where a pig is killed, dismembered, and its limbs are laid on the sick person, thereby identifying him with the slain victim. Further, it is possible that the grimmer rite of human sacrifice, implied, as we have seen, by Exod. xxii. 29, and confirmed by the evidence of excavation, for so the frequent occurrence of infant jar-burials has been interpreted, was also a part of the ritual of this dreadful night. It may, indeed, have been the original form of substitution sacrifice, and have given place later to the animal victim. The tradition of the slaying of the firstborn in Egypt points to some such element in the ritual. One would hesitate to suggest Egyptian influence on the form of the ritual, both because the connexion with Egypt is probably not original in the tradition of the feast, and because the form of the ritual finds sufficient explanation in the general character of the religious environment in which the early Hebrew form of this festival developed.

If we accept this interpretation of the significance of the eating of the victim, the reason for the injunction that none of the victim was to be left over becomes clear: anything left over would at once render invalid the magical and apotropaic value of the identification by destroying its completeness. This feature of substitution ritual is of frequent occurrence in the Babylonian incantation texts. The eating of bitter herbs belongs to the same category of ritual actions, and finds an illustration and an explanation in the Athenian spring festival of Anthesteria, a festival which has several interesting parallels to the ritual of the Hebrew Passover, and I have no doubt that both go back

[1] CT, xvii. 4 ff., Tab. N.

H

to the same source ultimately. During the three days of this festival the Athenians anointed their doors with pitch and chewed buckthorn, a plant, as Jane Harrison points out, of strong purgative properties. The days of the feast were fraught with danger, the spirits of the dead were abroad, and the pitch on the doors and the chewing of buckthorn were apotropaic measures, intended to protect the citizen against the baleful influence of the spirits.[1]

In the form in which we have the account of the institution and the ritual of the Passover, the transforming influence of Jahwism is manifest. It has become the commemorative ritual of Jahweh's crowning mercy, and all its details are coloured by the belief that they are a re-enactment of the original historical situation. But as soon as we free the ritual from these associations, it becomes clear that we have to do with an ancient festival whose rites fall into the same general category as those we have already seen in operation at the New Year Festival both in Mesopotamia and Canaan. It may be added that the regulations for smearing the side-posts and lintels with blood imply settled city life,[2] houses, not tents; also the argument that the lunar character of the feast, and the mention of kids or lambs as victims, implies a nomadic origin for the feast has little force. The whole Semitic stock of Mesopotamia and Canaan were originally nomads, but had long been assimilated to the culture already existing in the lands where they had settled. Lunar ritual was ancient in Babylonia millenniums before the Hebrews were heard of, and as far as that is concerned there is no reason why the lunar element in the Passover should not be Canaanite. We have already shown that the special significance of the kid or lamb belongs to the Babylonian incantation rituals, and need have no pastoral implications here.

[1] See J. S. Harrison, *Themis*, pp. 288–93 (1912).
[2] Mr. Sidney Smith reminds me that the Arabs carry out this piece of ritual, and that hence this prescription need not imply a settled mode of life. But while this form of the New Year ritual might have been adapted to nomad conditions, I am not satisfied that the Hebrew festival is of nomad origin.

But the third of the three early Hebrew festivals prescribed in the Book of the Covenant brings us up against
the problem of the Hebrew form of the New Year Festival
again.

This feast is called in our two early sources the feast of
Ingathering, and is a harvest or autumn festival. It is said
to be held *tequphath hashshanah* (J),[1] when the year has com-
pleted its 'circuit'; it is also said to be *beseth hashshanah*
(E),[2] 'at the going out of the year'. By what is now
generally recognized to be a mistranslation of the Hebrew,
both A.V. and R.V. render the words as 'the end of the
year'. But Buchanan Gray[3] showed long ago from the
analogy of the Accadian *sit šamši* that the phrase means the
'going out' of the year, in the same sense as the sun is said
to go out of his chamber; it is not the end of the year but
its beginning, the magical point when, the cycle being com-
pleted, the powers of nature begin anew to recreate the
world.

Hence we find here what we found in the earlier stages
of the New Year Festival in Mesopotamia, the occurrence
of a New Year Festival both in the spring and in the autumn.
Hebrew custom still retains this dual character of the New
Year celebration, holding its religious New Year in the
spring, and its civil New Year in the autumn.

We must, therefore, examine the ritual of this autumn
festival with the fact in mind that it was from the beginning
a New Year Festival.

As in the case of the Passover, no information as to the
nature of its ritual is given in the Book of the Covenant.
We must therefore again fall back upon the very full information contained in the Priestly Code, in Lev. xxiii. According to this source, the central rituals began on the 10th of
the seventh month, just as the Passover preparations began
on the 10th of the first month, and they continued until the

---

[1] Exod. xxxiv. 22.   [2] Exod. xxiii. 16.

[3] See G. Buchanan Gray, *Sacrifice in the Old Testament*, pp. 300–1
(1925).

21st, as in the case of the Passover. The order and nature of the constituent rituals are as follows:

(a) The Day of Atonement, whose ritual consisted of:
    i. The Scape-goat ritual,
    ii. The ritual purification of the priests, the people, the sanctuary, and the vessels of the cult.
    This initial ritual took place on the 10th of the month.

(b) The Feast of Tabernacles, on the 15th of the month. The ritual of this part of the festival consisted of the building of booths made of the leafy boughs of various trees, palms and willows being specially mentioned. The participants in the festival were to live in these booths for the seven days of the feast. Like the Passover it is associated by the Priestly legislators with the historical event of the Exodus. There is no reference to the keeping of this feast in pre-exilic times, and the account in Ezra iii. 4 is probably a doublet of the first genuine account of the holding of this festival in Neh. viii. 14. A reference in Zech. xiv. 16 ff. shows that the feast had become of considerable importance in the later pre-exilic period, and that it had either preserved or introduced a connexion of the ritual with the coming of the autumn rains.[1]

Further details of the way in which these two parts of the New Year ritual were carried out are found in the Mishnic treatises *Yoma*, *Sukkah*, and *Rosh hashshanah*. It is possible that these additional ritual details represent the survival of ancient elements which are passed over in silence by the Priestly editors. They may well be local variations discarded by those responsible for the organization of the Temple ritual. As in the case of the Passover, we have to do with the transformation of earlier forms of ritual under the influence of later Jahwism, and we see the same attempt to

---

[1] For a discussion of the significance of this festival see W. O. E. Oesterley, 'Early Hebrew Festival Rituals', in *Myth and Ritual*, pp. 111 ff.

connect the Feast of Tabernacles with the tradition of the Exodus. The people are to dwell in booths because Jahweh made their ancestors to dwell in tents when he brought them out of the land of Egypt (Lev. xxiii. 43).

Two elements in the Mishnic tradition concerning the Day of Atonement ritual call for notice, since they suggest some connexion with the Babylonian New Year ritual. The first is that it was, according to *Yoma*,[1] the custom for the first lot, by which the priestly duty of clearing the altar from ashes was assigned, to be decided by a foot-race up the altar ramp, a custom which was discontinued because one of the participants was injured in such a contest. This offers a parallel to the ʌoot-race in the Babylonian New Year Festival, symbolizing the victory of Nebo over Zu, a preliminary to the deliverance of Bel from the mountain.[2]

The second is that both the goats of the scape-goat ritual were decked with a fillet of red wool.[3] This recalls the two figurines, clothed in red garments, which were used with some propitiatory purpose in the preparatory stages of the Babylonian New Year Festival. Moreover, the use of the goats in this ritual strongly resembles the use of kids in a number of *puḫu*-rituals. A particularly interesting example is given by Ebeling.[4] Here the kid is said to be devoted to Ereškigal, and is ritually slain as a substitute for the offerer. The offerer's throat is struck by the priest with a wooden dagger, while the throat of the kid is cut with a copper dagger. The kid is then treated as a dead person, and buried with all the proper funeral rites.

Additional elements in the Feast of Tabernacles are also given by the Mishnah. Of these the most striking are the torch-dance,[5] the procession of priests,[6] and the water ritual,[7] all of which present parallels with Mesopotamian

---

[1] *Yoma*, ii. 1–2.   [2] *Epic of Creation* (ed. Langdon), pp. 45–7.
[3] *Yoma*, iv. 2.   [4] Ebeling, op. cit., pp. 67 ff.
[5] *Sukkah*, v. 2–3.   [6] *Sukkah*, v. 4.
[7] *Sukkah*, iv. 9.

or Canaanite ritual, and suggest, as in the case of the two elements of the Atonement ritual mentioned above, that they are survivals of ancient custom preserved in the Mishnic tradition.

The significance of the ritual of the booths made of greenery calls for special note. In the prelude to his code, Hammurabi states that among his other kingly and priestly duties it was his place to decorate the *gigunu* of Ai, the consort of Shamash, with greenery; and Gudea built a *gigunu* of cedar in the temple complex of E. NINNU at Lagash. In his discussion of the meaning of *gigunu*,[1] Mr. Sidney Smith has shown good grounds for supposing that the *gigunu* was a chamber used for the ritual of the sacred marriage. Hence it is permissible for us to suppose that the original significance of the booths of greenery was connected with the ritual of the sacred marriage, which, as we have seen, was one of the most important and frequently occurring features of both Mesopotamian and Canaanite ritual. The transformation of the ancient form of Hebrew ritual under the influence of Jahwism would naturally tend to obliterate this element from the ritual, but there are traces of its existence among the Hebrews in the mention of a goddess Anat-Jahu in the Elephantine Papyri,[2] implying a consort for Jahweh in the ritual of this outlying Hebrew settlement. It may also be inferred that the very frequent occurrence in the prophetic literature of the representation of the relation between Jahweh and Israel as that of husband and wife[3] bears indirect evidence to the existence of the sacred marriage as part of Hebrew ritual at an earlier period.

Hence, when we consider the various details of this third seasonal festival prescribed by the Book of the Covenant, a festival which is there said to be a New Year festival, we

[1] JRAS, 1928, pp. 849–68.
[2] See Sachau Papyri, no. 32. For a contrary view see A. van Hoonacker, Schweich Lectures, 1914, pp. 77–8.
[3] Cf. e.g. Jer. ii. 2; Ezek. xvi. 8; Hos. ii. 14–20: *et al.*

find abundant traces of ritual customs which bear a strong family resemblance to many of the elements which we have already found in the ritual of these civilizations which formed the Hebrews' earliest cultural environment.

We have a preparatory ritual of propitiation, accompanied by a confession and, in the case of the high priest, a laying-aside of official insignia, which has close parallels in the preparatory stages of the Babylonian New Year ritual. The same root *kpr* is used for the ritual purification of the shrine of the god with the carcass of a slaughtered sheep, as is used for the ritual purification performed by the high priest with blood of the slain goat in the shrine of Jahweh on the Day of Atonement.

The Mishnah has preserved the tradition of a ritual contest in the form of a foot-race, and the whole ritual of the scape-goat, with its obscure reference to the mysterious Azazel to whom the goat is devoted, bears a very close resemblance to Babylonian *puḫu*-rituals.

Then in the succeeding stages of the feast we have a ritual which suggests the early existence of a sacred marriage as part of the Hebrew New Year ritual. There are also traces of a sacred procession, and the work of Hans Schmidt, Mowinckel,[1] and others on the liturgical elements in the Psalter has shown that there are good grounds for supposing that this sacred procession, in which the king probably played an important part, led up to the central act of the New Year ritual, the enthronement of Jahweh. The preservation in the poetic literature of the Hebrews of the myth of Jahweh's conquest of the dragon, and the association of this event with the creation (cf. Ps. lxxiv. 12–17), suggests that some dramatic representation of this episode formed part of the proceedings in the early stage of the New Year ritual among the Hebrews. It has been recently suggested that the liturgical form of the story of creation in Gen. i points to its use by the priests as a chant

[1] Hans Schmidt, *Die Thronfahrt Jahves*, 1927 ; Sigmund Mowinckel, *Psalmenstudien*, i–v, 1921–4.

in a similar way to its use in the Babylonian New Year Festival.[1]

Thus in both forms of the New Year Festival among the Hebrews, in the spring and in the autumn, we have abundant evidence of close parallelism with the usages of this festival in Mesopotamia and in Canaan. The transforming influence of later Jahwism has almost entirely succeeded in obliterating the central elements of the dying and rising god, the sacred marriage, and the place of the king as the focus of the community's desires and emotions, but sufficient traces remain to show that all these elements once entered into the early Hebrew New Year ritual. Recent studies in the history of the kingship among the Hebrews have shown that, so far from having suffered a complete disappearance, the conception of the divine kingship as embodied in the person of the reigning king survived to quite a late period among the Hebrews.[2] We have already referred to the traces of the sacred marriage. The fact that as late as the time of Ezekiel the cult of Tammuz was connected with the Temple (Ezek. viii. 14) indicates the possibility of a popular identification of Jahweh with Tammuz. There is also an interesting passage in Hab. i. 12 which, according to an early Massoretic tradition, should read: 'Art not thou from everlasting, O Lord my God, mine Holy One, *thou* diest not.' It is possible to see in this passage a protest against popular ideas of a dying god. But this point will be referred to again in connexion with other forms of Hebrew ritual. It may, however, be added here that the figure of the Messianic King in later Jewish Apocalyptic represents the revival of the old conception of the divine king as the centre of the hopes of the community.[3]

[1] P. Humbert, RHPR, 1935, 'La relation de Genèse I et du Psaume 104 avec la liturgie du Nouvel-An israélite'.

[2] Cf. C. R. North in ZAW, 1932, 1, and A. R. Johnson, 'The Place of the King in the Jerusalem Cultus', in *The Labyrinth*, 1935.

[3] Cf. Hans Schmidt, *Der Mythos vom wiederkehrenden König im Alten Testament*, 1933.

We have devoted a good deal of time to the New Year ritual among the Hebrews with the object of showing that it was as central in the early Hebrew cultus as it was certainly among the Babylonians, and in all probability among the Canaanites. One last point may be dealt with before we pass on to other forms of Hebrew ritual. We have seen that political conditions in Mesopotamia produced a unification of the older forms of the New Year Festival, and that the form in which we have it now is that of an urban spring ceremony, in which the king has the central place, and the agricultural significance of the festival has receded into the background.

In Canaan, according to the evidence of the Ras Shamra tablets, there does not appear to have been the same unification of practice, and the texts suggest that while the same central ideas are dominant, the agricultural interests of the people produce the same distribution of the ritual occasions over the year as we find in early Hebrew practice. Hence the most probable inference from the close resemblance between the New Year ritual as it was practised in Mesopotamia, Canaan, and Israel, is that all three represent independent developments of a common central ritual, of which the Tammuz ritual may have been the earliest form. The close connexion of the three cultures, and the dominance of Babylonian culture in the Mediterranean area during the early part of the second millennium B.C., would naturally tend to the introduction of Babylonian elements into the ritual of Canaan and Israel, nor may Egyptian influence be ignored, as the Ras Shamra evidence shows. But the general impression gained from the early evidence is that in Canaan an independent form of the original pattern was worked out along lines that were determined by the character of the country, and that the Hebrews assimilated whatever religious elements they imported into the country to the main lines of the Canaanite ritual which they found there. Before the rise of the prophetic movement, Hebrew ritual was probably almost indistinguishable from that of Canaan, but the work of the prophets purged the religion of nearly all its ritual elements, and but for the labours of the priestly scribes after the Exile we should have had no foundation upon which to attempt the reconstruction of the ancient Hebrew ritual system.

The other seasonal feasts of the early stage of Hebrew religion only call for a passing mention, since we have very slight indications of the ritual connected with them. There is the Feast of Weeks, the Jewish *Shebuoth*, which has passed into the Christian calendar as Pentecost. This is the second of the three agricultural festivals prescribed in the Book of the Covenant. It took place at the beginning of the harvest, and from Lev. xxiii. 10, 15 we may infer that the central feature of this festival, and probably its oldest element, was a ritual connected with the first sheaf of the harvest. The various forms of this rite and its universal prevalence have been the subject of much study and are fully set out in the writings of Frazer, Mannhardt, and other anthropologists, and need not be discussed here.[1]

Then there are the two seasonal feasts which are generally mentioned together in the earlier literature, namely, new moon and sabbath. We know nothing of the ritual connected with these occasions, save that from a passage in 1 Sam. xx. 24–9 we gather that the new moon was a family feast. The constant association of the Sabbath with the new moon in the earlier literature suggests that in its earlier form the Sabbath was a lunar feast. We have already seen (Lecture I) that the Babylonians and Assyrians designated the 15th of the month, i.e. the day of the full moon, as *šabattum* or *šapattum*, and it seems most probable that in early Hebrew practice the two main crises of the moon were marked out as days of abstention from work, and as family feast days. The abstention from work on the

---

[1] See also the discussion of the significance of the ' wave-sheaf' in W. O. E. Oesterley, ' Early Hebrew Festival Rituals ', in *Myth and Ritual*, pp. 116–17; S. H. Hooke in ' Time and Custom ', *Folklore*, March 1937, pp. 11 ff.

seventh day is enjoined in the Book of the Covenant only for the periods of ploughing and harvest, and the rise of the seventh day of the week to paramount importance in the religious life of the Hebrews belongs to the later period of their history. We can see the emphasis on the Sabbath as a sign of the Covenant beginning with Ezekiel. In Isaiah's time new moons and sabbaths still come under the same joint condemnation.

As we are concerned here only with the early stage of the history of Hebrew ritual, we shall not discuss those seasonal festivals which enter into the later Jewish festal calendar, and are almost entirely connected with some historical event of later times. But several of these feasts contain elements which are certainly of early origin. The Feast of Purim, reflected in the late romance of the book of Esther, is interesting for us because it seems to represent a kind of doublet, a late echo, of the Babylonian New Year Festival, akin to the form in which it has survived in the Persian Sacaea, with its substitute king. The early elements in the Hanukkah festival will be discussed when we come to deal with dedication ritual further on. There is, however, one interesting feature which late Jewish literature has preserved, and which belongs to the earliest conceptions of the New Year Festival. The Mishnah associates New Year's Day with the divine judgement of mankind,[1] and the comment of the Mishnah is amplified in the Gemara. It can hardly be doubted that we have here another example of the preservation in the Mishnah of early elements in the seasonal festivals. It has already been pointed out that the ceremony of the fixing of destinies occupied an important place in the ritual of the Babylonian New Year Festival. We have the conception of this fixing of destinies in such cult-Psalms as Pss. lxxxv

[1] *Rosh Hashshanah*, i. 2. It is interesting to note that, according to the point of view here suggested, all the four occasions on which the world is judged, viz. Passover, Pentecost, New Year's Day, and Tabernacles, fall into the original pattern of the New Year Festival.

and cxxvi, where the *Wendung des Schicksals*, as Mowinckel terms it, the Hebrew *shubh shebhith*, the turning of fortune, is associated with other distinctive elements of the Hebrew New Year Festival.

We turn now to a festival which occupies an intermediate position between the Jewish seasonal festivals and the occasional rituals, namely, the feast of Dedication, the Hanukkah. In its later form it is clearly an institutional feast intended to celebrate the historical event of the dedication of the altar in the Temple at Jerusalem, in 165 B.C., after its profanation by Antiochus Epiphanes. The reason for describing it as occupying an intermediate position is based, first on its date, since it falls on the 15th of Chisleu, i.e. at the time of the winter solstice, and secondly on certain features of its ritual. As we know from the evidence of Josephus,[1] the festival was also known as the feast of Lights, or simply 'Lights'. This name arises from the most distinctive element in the ritual of the feast, namely, the kindling of lights. According to present Jewish usage the feast lasts eight days, and on each successive day an additional light is kindled, an order which follows the view of the School of Hillel as to the correct procedure. The School of Shammai, on the other hand, held that the full complement of lights should be kindled on the first night, and that the lights should be decreased by one on each succeeding night until the eighth night.

The increasing of the lights may point to an original solstitial ritual with the object of increasing the power of the sun as he begins to rise from the nadir of the winter's death. But Buchanan Gray's arguments against the existence of an original Hebrew festival at the winter solstice are too weighty to be set aside, and need not be repeated here.[2]

But there is a point arising from the nature of dedication

[1] *Ant.* xii. 7. 6, 7. For a full discussion of the significance of the lights at Hanukkah see O. S. Rankin, op. cit., c. 3.

[2] G. B. Gray, op. cit., pp. 290 f.

rituals and their connected myths in the Mesopotamian evidence and in the Ras Shamra texts which calls for notice in this connexion.

The second of the main groups of the Ras Shamra texts presented, as we saw, the appearance of a dedication ritual. It described the circumstances which led up to the building of a temple for Baal, the details of the building, a ritual which, if correctly interpreted, suggested the kindling of fires in the new sanctuary, and another ritual act, the opening of the window of the new temple, which was connected with the giving of rain. It concluded with the enthronement of Baal, a great feast with special sacrifices, to which the seventy sons of Asherat were invited, a sacred marriage, and the announcement by Baal of the destinies of Mot and Aleyan-Baal for the future. We have also pointed out the connexion of this Canaanite ritual with the myth in the Babylonian Creation Epic of the building of a temple for Marduk by the gods as a reward for his conquest of Tiamat. Hence there appears to have been a festival in Canaan, of a dedicatory nature, containing the main features of the New Year ritual, and probably celebrated in the autumn. Such a ritual might well have constituted the archetype for dedicatory rituals in Canaan, and the dedication of Solomon's temple may have presented features, now obliterated by the editorial process, borrowed from the Canaanite archetype. Moreover, when the necessity arose for providing a ritual in Maccabean times for the historical event already referred to, such a ritual would most probably assume a composite form, with features borrowed from the already existing tradition of the autumn New Year Festival, into which other elements may have entered which were survivals of early Canaanite custom.

There are many other occasional rituals, both public and private, in Hebrew religion, which suggest an early origin, but we cannot here deal with them in detail. One such ritual, of great importance in Hebrew religion, may be briefly discussed before we turn to the question of

sacrifice, and to our final summing up of the results of this
examination of the broad outlines of ritual among early
Semitic peoples.

This is the ritual of circumcision. The wide spread of
this custom, and the many forms which it has taken among
so-called primitive peoples, have been the object of considerable study among anthropologists, but we are merely
concerned here with the existence of the custom in Canaan
and among the Hebrews at an early period. The evidence
for the practice of the rite by the Phoenicians is given by
Ed. Meyer,[1] and Baudissin remarks that it was probably
originally some kind of dedication of the powers of pro-
creation, connected with the importance which the early
Semites attached to the idea of life and its symbols.[2]

But it may be possible to carry this view of the origin of
the rite a step further, and relate it to the main ritual
ideas which we have endeavoured to establish for early
Semitic ritual.

Hebrew tradition varies in its ascription of the origin of
the rite. By the Priestly editor it is attributed to Abraham
(Gen. xvii), by the Elohist to Joshua (Jos. v), and by the
Jahwist (Exod. iv. 22-6), to Zipporah, the Midianite wife
of Moses. The last passage, which has every sign of being
a very early tradition, connects the episode with the slaying of the firstborn of Pharaoh, the significance of which
we have already discussed in connexion with the Passover
ritual. In this rather obscure episode Jahweh appears as a
vengeful deity who seeks to slay Moses on account of some
ritual duty left unperformed. Zipporah propitiates Jahweh
by circumcising her son and performing a blood-ritual.
Ed. Meyer[3] has shown that the ritual was addressed to
Jahweh, with the words 'A bridegroom of blood art thou
to me', Zipporah thus intimating that she had become a
participant in the rite of the sacred marriage, and that
a substitution ritual had been duly performed by which the

[1] ZAW, xxix. 152.   [2] *Adonis und Eshmun*, p. 59 (1911).
[3] *Die Israeliten und ihre Nachbarstämme*, p. 59 (1906).

life of Moses was spared. Later on the original meaning of the ritual was completely lost, and circumcision became the sign of the covenant between Jahweh and Israel, but the fact that the non-observance of the rite carried with it the death-penalty (Gen. xvii. 14) is an indication of its ancient significance.

We turn now to the question of sacrifice, a ritual element which is so closely connected with the central conceptions which we have been considering that it cannot be rightly understood apart from these conceptions. It may seem somewhat superfluous to discuss a subject which has already been exhaustively dealt with by Robertson Smith, Buchanan Gray, Dussaud (for the theory of its Canaanite origin), and more recently, from the anthropological standpoint, by Professor E. O. James. But our purpose in these remarks is to treat sacrifice, not as a separate piece of ritual which can be explained on its own merits, but as a ritual which has arisen out of the central conceptions already referred to.

We have seen that the ritual killing of the king was one of the most important elements in the central religious occasion of the Semitic year, and that the king and the god came to be identified in this cult act at a very early period in the development of Semitic religion. We have also seen that at an early stage the practice arose of substituting a victim, human or animal, for the slain king-god. We have also pointed out the extension of this idea of substitution in many forms of incantation and exorcism rituals. Three main ideas underlie this early ritual of the slaying of the god in symbolic form. First, the idea of controlling the powers of nature in the interest of the community; second, the annual removal of ritual guilt and ill luck from the community by this ritual; third, the efficacy of a substitute victim, since, in the magical rituals, of which we have quoted several examples, the sufferer from the attack of an evil demon is delivered by being identified with the death and resurrection of the god in the form of a victim or other symbol, the kid, the well-known symbol of

Tammuz, being the commonest form of victim in these rituals.

Hence we have here a line of connexion between the ideas which found expression in these early forms of ritual, and certain ideas which are commonly recognized as implicit in the practice of sacrifice.

First, as a separation between the king, the priest, and the god, originally aspects of the same individual, takes place, the slaying of a victim, human or animal, assumes the form of a ritual act intended to induce or compel the favour of the god who controls those forces of nature which affect the well-being of the community. The priest becomes the individual who possesses the requisite knowledge for the correct performing of the ritual.

Second, the slaying of the victim and the ritual use of its blood acquires the purificatory efficacy of removing guilt or ritual defilement from a community, an individual, or a building.

Third, the idea of substitution, present both in the New Year ritual and in the incantation rituals, becomes a prominent element in the later Hebrew conception of sacrifice. We have seen[1] that there is early evidence in Egypt for the belief that by eating his slain predecessors the king could acquire their magical potency, and anthropology provides abundant illustration of this belief in many savage practices, but the general purpose of the identification of the offerer with the victim, symbolizing the god, in the field which we have been examining, seems to be substitution rather than communion. The object of the various ways in which identification could be effected was not that the offerer might partake of the life of the god, but that by symbolic participation in the death of the god he might secure the benefit of the magical consequences of that death. Hence, while Robertson Smith's central idea that the original purpose of sacrifice was a communal meal in which the participants by eating the flesh and blood of the god

[1] See p. 13.

absorbed his life may be found in those early Arab types of sacrifice upon which he bases his theory of the origin of sacrifice, it cannot be said that we find this conception in the field which we have been studying. We have seen that the Passover meal, which is generally taken as a survival of a nomad form of ritual among the Hebrews illustrating the idea of communion with the god, may be interpreted in an entirely different way.

It may therefore be legitimately assumed that the three main ideas of placation, of the ritual removal of guilt, and of substitution, characteristic of Hebrew burnt-offerings, sin-offerings, and trespass-offerings, have their source in the ideas underlying the central rituals of the New Year.

But there are other aspects of sacrifice whose origin seems to lie elsewhere. When the god came to be regarded as the owner of the land, and as dwelling in a temple, surrounded by an organized body of priests and temple servants, his title was acknowledged by offerings from flocks and herds and from the fruits of the soil, and the fiction was kept up that the gods needed their daily meals. In the Babylonian ritual texts provision is made for the 'great meal' and the 'little meal', *petit déjeuner*, so to speak, and in this way the maintenance of the temple staffs was secured. We have lists of various kinds of animal offerings, wines, oil, bread, and everything necessary for the table of the gods. One of the earliest tablets from Ras Shamra to be deciphered contained such a list. The principle was capable of large extension, and hence arose the class of offerings, unconnected with the three main ideas of placation, purification, and substitution, designated by the generic term *minhah*, or *mattanah*. Such offerings were gifts, not entirely voluntary, but arising from the nature of the relation between the god and the worshipper, and intended to maintain that relation in a satisfactory state. Hence while Buchanan Gray is quite right when he points out that none of the specific Hebrew terms except *nedarim* imply the idea of a gift to the god, it is clear that, historically, all the specific types of offering belong to one of two main classes, whether they are slain, burnt, eaten in part by the offerer, or merely presented in the presence of the god. They are either offerings which have their origin in the central rite of the slaying of the god and the ideas connected therewith, or they are in essence gifts, given no doubt in recognition of the due claims of the god and his entourage, but, even though they aim at securing the favour of the god, still retaining the character of gifts, *mattanoth*, whether slain, burnt in part, eaten in part, by priest or worshipper.

Before leaving the subject of sacrifice, we have to discuss the evidence of the Ras Shamra texts concerning sacrifice and its terminology among the Canaanites.

We have already seen that sacrifices entered into the dedicatory ritual of the temple of Baal, and included animals, such as asses, for instance, which were not used for sacrifice by the Hebrews. In the first text to be translated, a list of temple offerings, we find prescribed for various gods and temple officials such offerings as sheep, bulls, heifers, lambs, doves, and birds. Another of the earlier texts describes a type of fertility offering which seemed to find a concrete illustration in the discovery at Minet el-beida of a deposit of jars laid out in rows in a pit to which stone or pottery conduits led. Virolleaud's translation of the text runs : 'Place the pots in the ground. Pour into the heart (liver) of the ground the *slm*. Pour into the heart of the fields the *arbdd*. If you do this, your tree will be with me.'[1] In the long text, I AB, containing the myth of the death of Aleyan-Baal, a god who is about to be slain (it is not clear whether it is Mot or Aleyan-Baal who speaks) says, 'I am the lamb given as a *kll* with pure wheat'.

For the technical terms we find in the texts, *slm*, Hebrew *shelamim* ; *dbh*, the generic Hebrew *zebakh*, slain sacrifice ; *est*, Hebrew *'ishsheh*, fire-offering ; *kll*, Hebrew *kalil*, holocaust ; *asm*, Hebrew *asham* ; *qdmt*, the equivalent of the Hebrew *bikkurim*, first-fruits. These specific terms are of

[1] *Syria*, xiii, 1, pp. 11–13 (1932).

considerable importance in that they show that the types of offerings which they denote existed in Canaan in the fourteenth century B.C., and therefore can hardly have been invented by the post-exilic priestly writers.

The general impression given by the relation of the sacrifices to the rituals as a whole is that the people of Ras Shamra at the period of the texts were in much the same stage of ritual development as the Hebrews in the pre-prophetic period of their religious history. We only know the Hebrew ritual in a form in which the old central rituals have disappeared, and, although the seasonal occasions persist, the old dramatic ritual has been replaced by sacrifices whose character has been derived from the ideas underlying the cult acts representing the passion and resurrection of the god.

We can see that all this still existed in full strength at Ras Shamra, although not in the same unified form as in the later Babylonian ritual, and there is good ground for believing that a form of ritual closely akin to that of Ras Shamra in its main outlines and intention prevailed among the Hebrews in the early period of their settlement in Canaan. Whether they borrowed these main outlines from their neighbours together with the terminology of the sacrifices, adapting their borrowings to the worship of their own god, Jahweh; or whether both peoples received the substance of this type of religion from their common ancestors in south Palestine, as Dussaud would have us believe,[1] cannot be determined from the evidence at present available. But we can at least acknowledge that the light which this new material has thrown upon the environment of the Hebrews at the time when they were settling down in Palestine, makes it probable that we are not wholly astray in attempting to reconstruct the outline, still all too faint, of early Hebrew religion along the lines of the general pattern which we have found existing in Mesopotamia and in Canaan.

[1] But see now R. Dussaud, *Les Découvertes de Ras Shamra et l'Ancien Testament*, pp. 112-113 (1937).

To accept such a view, if only provisionally, of the beginnings of Hebrew religion does no wrong to its later majestic unfolding. Rather does it enhance the wonder of the achievement of those Hebrew seers to acknowledge 'the rock whence they were hewn and the hole of the pit whence they were digged'. There can hardly be a nobler fruit of spiritual insight than to have transformed the conception of a dying god and a sacred marriage into the vision of the Suffering Servant of Jahweh, and of an inward union between a people and their God which could find expression in the noble words 'thy Maker is thine husband', and again, 'I have loved thee with an everlasting love'.

APPENDIX
RAS SHAMRA BIBLIOGRAPHY

THE *editio princeps* of the texts, consisting of a transcription and French translation, is contained in the series of reprints from *Syria* covering the campaigns at Ras Shamra from 1929 to 1935. Here will be found all the Aleyan-Baal poems and the other texts discussed in these lectures. In addition, since these lectures were delivered, M. Virolleaud has published the first two volumes of a series entitled *Mission de Ras Shamra*, containing further texts of great importance, namely, *La Légende Phénicienne de Danel* and *La Légende de Keret, Roi des Sidoniens*. It is impossible to overestimate the debt which we owe to M. Virolleaud for this vast work of careful scholarship. The number of books, articles, and discussions arising out of this preliminary publication of the texts increases daily, and the following list makes no claim to completeness, being only intended to help students of the texts to find the more important contributions to the interpretation of the texts.

ALBRIGHT, W. F. New Light on Early Canaanite Language and Literature, BASOR, April 1933.

More Light on the Canaanite Epic of Aleyan-Baal and Mot, BASOR, April 1933.

The North-Canaanite Epic of Aleyan-Baal and Mot, JPOS, 1932.

The North-Canaanite Poems of Aleyan-Baal, JPOS, 1934.

A New Hebrew Literature in Cuneiform, *Jewish Forum*, March 1934.

The Canaanite God Hauron (Horon), AJSL, 1936.

New Canaanite Historical and Mythological Data, BASOR, Oct. 1936.

Zabul Yam and Thapit Nahar in the Combat between Baal and the Sea, JPOS, 1936.

BARTON, G. A. A North Syrian Poem on the Conquest of Death, JAOS, 1932.

A Liturgy for the Spring Festival at Jerusalem, JBL, 1934.

The Second Liturgical Poem from Ras Shamra, JAOS, 1935.

BAUER, H. Entzifferung der Keilschrifttafeln von Ras Schamra, 1930.

Das Alphabet von Ras Schamra, 1932.

Die Gottheiten von Ras Schamra, ZAW, 1933.

Die Gottheiten von Ras Schamra, ii, ZAW, 1935.

Die alphabetischen Keilschrifttexte von Ras Schamra, 1936.

BURROWS, E. Origin of the Ras Shamra Alphabet, JRAS, 1936.

CANTINEAU, J. La Langue de Ras Schamra, *Syria*, 1932.

DHORME, E. Première traduction des textes phéniciens de Ras Shamra, *Revue Biblique*, 1930.

A propos des textes hippiatriques de Ras Shamra, *Syria*, 1934.

La Lettre d'Ewir-shar, *Syria*, 1934.

DIRINGER, D. Il nuovo alfabeto semitico di Ras Samrah, *Biblica*, 1934.

DUSSAUD, R. Note additionelle, *Syria*, 1929.

Brèves remarques sur les tablettes de Ras Shamra, *Syria*, 1931.

La Mythologie phénicienne d'après les tablettes de Ras Shamra, RHR, 1931.

Le Sanctuaire et les dieux phéniciens de Ras Shamra, RHR, 1932.

Les Phéniciens au Negeb et en Arabie d'après un texte de Ras Shamra, RHR, 1933.

Ba'al et Ben-Dagon dans les textes de Ras Shamra, *Syria*, 1934.

Le Mythe de Ba'al et d'Aleyan d'après les documents nouveaux, RHR, 1934.

Note, *Syria*, 1935.

Deux stèles de Ras Shamra portant une dédicace au dieu Dagon, *Syria*, 1935.

Les Éléments déchaînés, *Syria*, 1935.

A propos de la Table dite généalogique, *Syria*, 1935.

Le vrai nom de Ba'al, RHR, 1936.

Les Découvertes de Ras Shamra et l'Ancien Testament, 1937.

EBELING, E. Zur Entstehungsgeschichte des Keilschriftalphabets von Ras Schamra, *Sitzungsber. Berlin. Akad., Phil.-Hist. Kl.*, 1934.

EISSFELDT, O. Baal Zaphon, Zeus Casios und der Durchzug der Israeliten durchs Meer, 1932.

Die religionsgeschichtliche Bedeutung der Funde von Ras Schamra, *Forschungen und Fortschritte*, 1932.

Eine antike literarische Bezeugung des Ras Schamra-Alphabets, *F. u. F.*, 1934.

Die Wanderung palästinisch-syrischer Götter Ost und West, JPOS, 1934.

Die religiongeschichtliche Bedeutung der Funde von Ras Schamra, ZDMG, 1934.

FRIEDRICH, J. Zu den drei Aleph-Zeichen des Ras Schamra Alphabets, ZA, 1933.

GASTER, T. H. The Combat of Death and the Most High, JRAS, 1932.

The Combat of Aleyan-Baal and Mot, JRAS, 1934, seq.; id. 1935.

The Ritual Pattern of a Ras Shamra Epic, AO, 1933.

An Ancient Semitic Mystery Play, *Studi e Materiali delle Religioni*, 1934.

The Story of Aqhat, id. 1936.

The Earliest Known Miracle Play, *Folklore*, 1933.

The Chronology of Palestinian Epigraphy, PEFQS, 1935.

The Harrowing of Baal, *Acta Orientalia*, 1937.

The Battle of the Rain and the Sea, *Iraq*, 1937.

GINSBERG, H. L. Notes in OLZ, 1934, 1935, and 1936.

The Ugarit Texts, 1936.

GINSBERG, H. L., and MAISLER, B. Semitized Hurrians in Syria and Palestine, JPOS, 1934.

GORDON, C. H. A Marriage of the Gods in Canaanite Mythology, BASOR, Feb. 1937.

GRAHAM, W. C., and MAY, H. G. Culture and Conscience, 1935.

HARRIS, Z. S. A Hurrian Affricate or Sibilant, in Ras Shamra, JAOS, 1935.

The Structure of Ras Shamra C, JAOS, 1934.

HROZNÝ, B. Une Inscription hurrite de Ras Schamra en langue hurrite, AO, 1932.

Les Ioniens à Ras Schamra, AO, 1932.

JACK, J. W. The Ras Shamra Tablets: Their Bearing on the Old Testament, 1935.

MAISLER, B. A Genealogical List from Ras Shamra, JPOS, 1936.

MONTGOMERY, J. A. Notes on the Mythological Texts from Ras Shamra, JAOS, 1933.

Ras Shamra Notes II, JAOS, 1934.

       „   „   „   III, JAOS., 1935.
       „   „   „   IV, JAOS, 1935.
       „   „   „   V, JAOS, 1936.

Oracle Place Names, JBL, 1935.

MONTGOMERY, J. A., and HARRIS, Z. S. The Ras Shamra Mythological Texts, 1935.

NAISH, J. P. The Ras Shamra Tablets, PEFQS, 1932.

OLMSTEAD, A. T. Excursus on the Alphabet of Ras Shamra, in *The Alphabet*, ed. M. Sprengling, 1931.

SAYCE, A. H. Etruscan Affinities in a Ras Shamra Tablet, JRAS, 1932.

SCHAEFFER, C. F. A. The reports on the successive campaigns at Ras Shamra from 1929 up to the present date, published in *Syria*, 1929, 1931, 1932, 1933, 1934, 1936. Also articles in the *Illustrated London News*, 2 Nov. 1929; 29 Nov. 1930; 21 Nov. 1931; 12 Mar. 1932; 11 Feb. 1933; 3 Mar. 1934; 16 Feb. 1935; 27 April 1935; 20 Feb. 1937; in *L'Illustration*, 12 Oct. 1929; 29 Nov. 1930; 21 Nov. 1931; 11 Feb. 1933; 3 Mar. 1934; and in the *National Geographical Magazine*, Oct. 1930; July 1933.

VIROLLEAUD, C. *Editio princeps* of the text and translation of the Ras Shamra Texts in *Syria* from 1929 to the present date.

WILLIAMS, W. G. The Ras Shamra Inscriptions and their Significance for the History of Religion, AJSL, 1935.

INDEX

www.ingramcontent.com/pod-product-compliance
Lightning Source LLC
Chambersburg PA
CBHW071105090426

42737CB00013B/2487